Anderson's Legacy

*The First Fifty Years of Belcan Corporation
and Its Worldwide Impact*

Producer: Bruce Richardson
Assistant Editor: Patsi B. Trollinger
Photographer: Ben Richardson
Copy Editor: Freear Williams

BENJAMIN PRESS
PO Box 100
Perryville KY 40468
www.BenjaminPress.com

ISBN 978-0-9793431-8-6

Printed in China through Four Colour Imports

Anderson's Legacy

*The First Fifty Years of Belcan Corporation
and Its Worldwide Impact*

Text by Margaret A. Lane
Photography by Ben Richardson

Great Leaders of America Series by
BENJAMIN PRESS

Foreword

Tribute from a Friend: 'He is a man of character'

In the top ten of all the men I have known, including kings and presidents, Ralph G. Anderson would be included. His humility and honesty have given him the fine reputation he so richly deserves. He is a man of character. He is a man of integrity. He is a precious man. He calls me his "younger brother."

Spiritual values made his marriage to Ruth one of the most special I have known. One night as I was visiting in his living room, I thought that no other couple's faces made such happy sounds as those of Ralph and Ruth. . .only happy sounds that generate energy and positive enthusiasm for life.

When Ralph G. Anderson looks at you, he will have his head held straight, a twinkle in his eye, and positive energy radiating in his face.

Ralph Anderson's creativity brought Belcan Corporation into existence. Best wishes for a wonderful 50th anniversary to one of the world's finest engineering firms, to whom all of us are indebted.

June 2008
Robert H. Schuller
Founding Pastor
Crystal Cathedral Ministries

Anderson's Legacy

The Anderson Saga

Milk cows and scruffy lambs provide lessons in labor

Scruffy-looking lambs may seem unlikely components for building a successful multimillion dollar corporation, but they were enough to set Ralph G. Anderson on the right path. Born on a Mercer County farm in midsummer 1923, Ralph Gilbert Anderson quickly learned that every member of his family had chores to do. In his earliest memories, Ralph was the kid who carried water from the spring and gathered coal and kindling to feed the fireplaces. It did not take long for him to figure out that work had value.

"I became interested in making money," he recalls, "so I started taking the lambs that our old ewe wouldn't accept. I learned that I could feed them on a bottle and raise them to be adults, and then I could breed more sheep to sell. People began to call me 'Buck' or 'Bucksheep.' Looking back, I guess my sheep were a business, although I didn't realize it at the time."

Photo, opposite page: Ralph G. Anderson celebrated his 1950 college graduation with parents, William Robert (Mr. Bob), and Mattie Jane Cunningham Anderson. His childhood home (right) is located on Warwick Road near Harrodsburg. Ralph keeps these images at his desk to remind him of his roots.

That instinct for business would eventually prompt Anderson to found Belcan Corporation, one of the nation's largest engineering firms. Belcan is a complex and vast operation, but much of its success can be traced back to the entrepreneurial spirit that its owner showed as a young farm boy. Early in life, Ralph learned that honest labor yielded results.

"My father raised a half acre of tobacco, worked at Kentucky Utilities, and managed the local

tobacco warehouse during the winter," Ralph says. "He saved up $1,500, bought our seven-acre farm on Warwick Road in Mercer County, and built a house. My niece owns it now."

Ralph has detailed memories of life on the farm. "We kept a big garden, raised chickens and turkeys, and had a couple of cows. At mealtime, we ate a lot of chicken and vegetables from the garden. Our house had kerosene lights until I was about seven years old. That's when electricity came to the area."

The modern conveniences made life a little easier, but Anderson's father had strong convictions about old-fashioned labor. Ralph vividly recalls being rebuked by his father one day. "Ralph," he said bluntly, "if you can't milk a cow or strip tobacco, you'll never amount to anything." The judgment left Ralph feeling the need to prove himself.

"My father had shocked me and I went to see a neighbor, Mr. Deshazer, about working on his 100-acre farm. I asked him a question. 'If I do a man's job, could I get a man's salary?' He agreed

EDNA
Girl Reserve '38-'41; Freshman Home Room V. Pres.
Glee Club '38, '39; Home Room V. Pres.

Best
Pauline

HENRY CLAY DAVENPORT
Hi-Y '38, '39; Bible Study '38, '39; Glee
Club '38, '39; Safety Patrol '41; Jr. Ky.
Acad. Science '40; H.A.A. '38-'40.

RALPH GILBERT ANDERSON
H.A.A. '38-'41; Hi-Y '38, '39; Bible Study
'38, '39; Football '39, '40; H-Club '40;
Typist Harrodian '41.

to pay me one dollar a day if I worked from sunup to sundown. He must have been happy with me, because I eventually earned two dollars a day."

Ralph was twelve years old at the time, and the nation was gripped by the Great Depression, but he focused on what he knew best – hard work and farm life. He continued working for Deshazer all through high school and earned a reputation as one of the region's fastest tobacco cutters. "I could cut a thousand sticks a day," Ralph says.

His success stemmed in part from the fact that he took pleasure in doing most of his tasks. "I enjoyed working on the farm. We put up hay using a team of horses because we didn't have tractors, and

---

Ralph's father told him 'If you can't milk a cow or strip tobacco, you'll never amount to anything.'

we thinned the rows of corn by hand. I always understood that a person can't be afraid of hard work. There's no way to get along if you goof off."

While in eighth grade, Anderson wrote in an essay that he wanted to become an engineer. Years later, he confessed that he thought engineering was all about driving a train, yet his school records show an affinity for the subject most crucial in engineering – mathematics. While Anderson was an average student in most of his classes, he maintained a remarkable 99.9 percent average in math at Harrodsburg High School.

Farm work and wages took a back seat any time school was in session, but Anderson's life still was filled with physical demands. Instead of riding a bus, he ran two miles to school each day. After classes ended, he practiced with the football team and then ran the two miles back home.

Ralph and his sister, Gladys, with a pet rooster on the family farm.

11

Photos, clockwise beginning left: Aviation pioneers Orville and Wilbur Wright are among Ralph G. Anderson's ancestors, as is frontiersman Daniel Boone (above). The Fort Harrod historic site in Harrodsburg, Ky., honors explorer James Harrod, who founded the settlement and welcomed Anderson's forebearer, Cornelius Cozine, as one of the early settlers. By the time Ralph was a young boy, the Andersons were firmly established in farming near Harrodsburg.

Daniel Boone and Other Interesting Relatives

Ralph G. Anderson can trace his pioneer lineage back to Daniel Boone, the intrepid frontiersman who helped open Kentucky to westward expansion from the original colonies. Thanks to Boone and the fearless James Harrod, Mercer County's Harrodsburg was the first permanent English settlement west of the Appalachian Mountains. It was Harrod himself who welcomed the Reverend Cornelius Cozine of Pennsylvania into the fledging settlement. Cozine thrived in the backwoods and became the great, great, great grandfather of Ralph Anderson and another venerable Mercer Countian, Frances Keightly Moseley. She and Ralph are proud of saying, "We've been here since Harrod."

"Wayne Dyer says if you go back far enough, we're all cousins." (Dyer is a highly regarded motivational speaker whose lectures and tapes have become an inspiration to Ralph Anderson.)

Wrong Job, Right Girl

One outcome of Ralph's school days was a friendship with John Harris that lasted for many years. The two met while in seventh grade, and both later played sports at Harrodsburg High School. They moved to Cincinnati in the fall of 1941 after graduating and worked for the Curtiss-Wright aircraft company, where Ralph's duties involved cutting gears. In a relatively short period of time, he managed to improve the gear-cutting process, resulting in a stronger product.

In a curious twist of history, recent genealogical research has linked the Anderson family to Wilbur and Orville Wright, aviation pioneers who helped found the Curtiss-Wright Corporation.

Although Anderson may have been a good fit at Curtiss-Wright, he felt compelled to join the Air Force in 1943 to help with the war effort. "I was in the Air Force from March of 1943 until November of 1946," he says. "Near the end of navigation school, when I needed only one more flight, I got word that they couldn't pass me. Disappointed, I went into bombardier

school and became a B-29 flight engineer. That test wasn't easy – you had to disassemble a propeller blindfolded – but I passed it."

At war's end, Ralph discovered that his experience in navigation school may have happened for the best. "There had been seven cadets named Anderson enrolled in flight school, and all of them went to England and were killed. I had letters from their wives and families after that."

Anderson enrolled at the University of Cincinnati in 1946, courtesy of the GI Bill. He also worked as a co-op student at Armco Steel in Middletown, Ohio, but even that was not enough to cover the cost of tuition. Aware of Kentucky's in-state tuition rate, he transferred to the University of Kentucky where he worked as a student instructor in the machine shop, earning $40 a month. Ralph G. Anderson earned a mechanical engineering degree from the University of Kentucky in August 1950.

The time at Armco Steel had a long-lasting effect on Anderson. That was where he met a talented young woman named Ruth May Tucker, a Middletown girl who worked as a bookkeeper in the canteen. The couple married on March 27, 1948, and found a place to live on South Limestone Street in Lexington. Ralph discovered he had found a hard-working partner.

"Ruth worked at the Greyhound station for $25 a week," he says, "and helped put me through school. We were a team from then on."

Blessed with a strong background in bookkeeping, Ruth became the financial specialist for the couple. She took a detailed approach to dealing with numbers; Ralph preferred to keep approximations in his head.

Ruth is shown here in 1948 preparing to cut the cake at her bridal shower. A new toaster was one of the many gifts received as she began married life with Ralph G. Anderson.

More Intuition than Planning

Thousands of former GIs were seeking work in 1950, and Ralph knew that job-hunting would not be easy. He mailed one hundred resumes and received one offer from the Barber-Coleman Corporation in Rockford, Illinois. He accepted, and he and Ruth moved their carload of belongings.

Later that fall, while Ralph was driving back to UK for a football game, he was involved in an automobile accident in Indianapolis. Recuperating at the home of a friend, Ralph learned about a job in Dayton, Ohio, with the Frigidaire Division of General Motors. He decided to take the job, setting off a series of work experiences that proved instrumental in shaping his views about business and innovation.

"I worked at General Motors in Dayton for a year," Ralph explains, "then switched to General Electric in Evendale, where I tested engines."

The task was a good match for Ralph's knowledge and skills; the management style was not. "I couldn't get myself geared up to work there," he admits, "and I finally decided it was time to move on." Undaunted, Ralph retained the conviction that everything in life happens for the best. He focused on acquiring business contacts and learning from every new situation, whether or not it was ideal.

By the early 1950s, Ralph's business philosophy was taking shape. He felt certain that the most effective forms of management focus on person-to-person dealings, not on a bureaucratic maze of departments. Ralph became utterly convinced that the heart of management lies in people.

He smiles as he recalls that era in his life. "I had no plan but plenty of intuition. At GE, I was working in a hot factory environment and couldn't breathe. I would go outside, sit down, and say to myself 'Man, I wish I had my own business.'"

> "I would go outside,
> sit down, and say
> to myself 'Man, I wish
> I had my own business.'"

Anderson was sure that his future involved owning a business, but the time wasn't right to take a big financial risk. He and Ruth were ready to start a family, and they needed a steady income. In 1953, Ralph took a job with the Kett Corporation, an engineering specialty firm. As one of six project managers, he helped coordinate the work of seventy engineers.

At Kett, Ralph acquired expertise in stress analysis on turbo jet engine frames and also learned about analytical work, design, and sales. He had the unique opportunity to observe the operations of a small technical service engineering company, and he saw firsthand how the company benefited because the owner, Karl Schakel, gave his workers the freedom to utilize their skills and creativity.

Ralph also developed contacts with Allison Gas Turbines and GE Aviation, and he formed a friendship with engineer Jack Hope that would enrich their lives for more than four decades.

Years later, entrepreneurial expert Joe Massie would write in his book, *Anderson's Way*: "All the tendencies toward entrepreneurship were present in Anderson from boyhood. All that was

(continued on page 21)

From the Jalopy to the Mercedes: A Formula for Speed

Look deep into the branches of Ralph Anderson's family tree and you'll find some famous cousins named Wilbur and Orville Wright. The pair began their professional lives with an obsession for bicycles and concluded it by making aviation history.

As a child, Ralph could never quite afford a bicycle, but he and some friends used part of an old buggy to career downhill on dusty farm roads. Later the boys got hold of a jalopy. "We took everything off a Model T except the engine and seat," Ralph says. "The other fellows would sit on the frame, and I'd drive." A 20-cent gallon of gas gave the boys miles of speed and freedom.

Ralph was a grown man before he owned a car. "In 1942, I bought a 1934 four-door Ford. It was nothing but a wreck, so when I went into the service, I just parked it on the lot at Curtiss-Wright and left it."

Back in school in Cincinnati after the war, Ralph depended on streetcars to get to class. After moving to Lexington, he and Ruth saved enough money to buy a new Chevrolet.

The Chevrolet was followed by Cadillacs, and by 1984, Ralph was ready to splurge. "I had a good year and bought a Rolls Royce for $165,000," he says with a laugh.

To keep things even at home, Ralph spent an equal amount on a twelve-carat diamond ring for Ruth. He now admits that the jewelry may have been a wiser purchase.

Another family member who benefited from Ralph G. Anderson's love for speed was daughter Candace. She recalled that, as a 16-year-old, she dreamed of driving a Volkswagen Beetle. However, after receiving advice and encouragement from her father,

Candace left the dealership driving a 1972 bright orange Corvette. According to Candace, her father considered it his duty to "blow the carbon out of the powerful machine every weekend."

In recent years, Ralph's auto purchases have turned out more favorably. He has owned a series of Mercedes 600's, always black, and has delighted in every one. "The dealer says not to hit speeds higher than 35 for the first thousand miles, but I say open them up."

Now in his 80's, Ralph's latest Mercedes has a twelve-cylinder engine and dual turbo chargers. Ralph was hospitalized when the car was due to be delivered. "They called and said the car was up in Baltimore, and they had installed a racing engine. I've had it up to 140 miles per hour."

> "We took everything off
> a Model T except the engine
> and seat. The other fellows would
> sit on the frame, and I'd drive."

Ralph's love affair with cars and innovative technology has influenced decisions regarding corporate sponsorships at Belcan Corporation.

The company recently has supported two programs involving engineering students and automobile design. At the University of Kentucky, Belcan funds have helped students develop Gato Del Sol III, a car fueled by solar

panels. At Brigham Young University in Utah, engineering students are part of a worldwide program known as PACE (Partners for the Advancement of Collaborative Engineering Education), which offers the challenge to design and construct a next-generation formula race car. At both locations, Belcan funds and expertise have aided student participants.

Photo left: Ralph checks out the experimental car he helped fund as a project for engineering students at the University of Kentucky. Above: Ralph also has supported student work at Brigham Young University on a next-generation race car.

With a positive attitude,
we can meet our goals,
if we don't care who gets the credit.

from the Belcan Charter

needed, to use aircraft engineering jargon, was a short thrust from an afterburner to push Anderson away from working for other corporations into forming his own firm." Massie believes that having Schakel as a role model provided that crucial boost to Ralph's plans.

When Kett created a spin-off company, Ketco, and decided on a Florida location, sales manager Ralph realized that he didn't like bugs, sun, and sand. He and Ruth purchased a home on Pendery Drive in Cincinnati and welcomed Candace, their daughter, on March 1, 1956.

Cincinnati, shown here in a night photo taken along the banks of the Ohio River, is home to Belcan Corporation.

A Habitual Sense of Optimism

Ralph G. Anderson's intuition told him the time had arrived for him to start his own company. In terms of national and international events, his sense of timing was excellent. America was caught up in a postwar tidal wave of innovation, and the Sputnik era was soon to begin, thrusting engineers into even greater limelight. Cincinnati was a hotspot, known as a center of aviation and industrial technology.

The time was right, but Ralph had no capital and meager savings. Commercial banks might have little reason to support an unknown, unproven engineer in search of a loan. From the perspective of most bankers, Ralph was a man without assets.

Yet he did, in fact, have much of what he needed to succeed in business. A potential investor willing to look beyond the obvious would see that Anderson possessed a remarkable reservoir of knowledge and had an excellent reputation within the engineering community. He also

possessed intangible qualities that could not be purchased with any amount of money. Ralph was marked by a habitual sense of optimism that prompted him to view adversity as a challenge and misfortune as a possible opportunity. He had a sure conviction that he did not fit into larger corporations.

Ralph had a remarkable ability to learn from every situation, whether good or bad, and he found ideas for improvement on every engineering job. He was willing to try new ideas because he held a deep-seeded belief that he could control his future more effectively by 'doing his own thing.'

Along with every good trait that had marked him since his days as a farm boy – and every piece of knowledge he had gained on the job– Ralph had three other things that made him unbeatable. First, he had mastered a direct, personal approach to solving business problems that gave him a natural advantage over the

bureaucratic, impersonal approaches of large corporations. He had a strong ally, his wife, who was supportive in all endeavors. And he had a gem of an idea for the type of business that would mesh perfectly with his particular skills and convictions: a specialty engineering company that could provide highly skilled services to industrial firms on a temporary basis. This concept would blossom into the original mission of the Belcan Corporation.

Ralph G. Anderson's daughter, Candace McCaw, is shown here with her family. Left to right: Jason, Amanda, Candace, Michael, and Matthew McCaw.

Belcan Corporation

A global business begins with a one-room office and fresh cookies on a Saturday morning

Intuition may have told Ralph that the time was right for him to form his own company, but he still needed money. He and Ruth took out a second mortgage on their house and borrowed money from friends. Ralph was confident that every cent would be repaid. "I knew I could pump gas if I had to."

Still short of the needed start-up capital, he headed back to his hometown. "I talked to folks in Harrodsburg, and a few of them said, 'Whatever you do, don't go see Ott Elliott.' Ott was a neighbor of ours, and some people thought he was a religious nut. But I went to see him, and he asked me how much I needed. I couldn't think, so I just said $7,000. Ott wrote me a check. He didn't want any interest, so I told him that I'd donate the interest to the church."

Apparently that was exactly what Ott wanted to hear. As Ralph explains in a phrase popular

> "He didn't want any interest, so I told him that I'd donate the interest to the church."

in rural Kentucky: "That tickled the life out of him."

Ralph G. Anderson was 35 at the time he filed documents of incorporation for the business in 1958. One of the toughest assignments was coming up with a name for the new entity. Ruth found a solution. "Our daughter's name is Candace, and she had a friend named Belinda. Stick part of their names together, and you get Belcan." The name proved to have just the right sound of strength and dependability.

The company name turned out to be just one of Ruth's crucial contributions to the business. In the early days, she was the company's office manager and bookkeeper, as well as Ralph's partner in decision-making. His penchant for creativity and risk-taking was matched by her detail-oriented mind that grasped the value of organization and managerial controls. Together, they made a potent team.

The pair succeeded, according to business expert Joe Massie, by employing complementary skills.

(continued on page 25)

The Ideal Partner

Ralph's first and best business partner was his wife, Ruth. Born in Middletown, Ohio, Ruth May Tucker was working as a bookkeeper in the canteen of Armco Steel when she met Ralph Anderson, who came in every morning for pecan pie and coffee.

According to corporate legend, the first five Belcan employees visited the Andersons' home on Saturday mornings to enjoy Ruth's homemade chocolate chip cookies while collecting their paychecks.

The Belcan Charter

By 1970, Ralph G. Anderson and his Belcan team had formalized a Belcan Charter that clearly stated the corporation's commitment to excellence in serving customers. The Charter was etched onto standing desk plaques and distributed to every Belcan office. Employees then and now have proudly used the tenets of the charter when introducing Belcan's services to potential customers.

Belcan Corporation provides a full range of engineering services to clients in a wide variety of industries. The following set of principles will guide our business activities.

- Belcan is committed to excellence; dedicated to the customer and customer service and respect for the individual. Belcan's greatest assets are its people.

- Belcan employees should keep sales number one in mind. Any action of any employee will affect sales.

- Belcan will be a market driven organization.

- To make Belcan grow, we will supply the tools to do the job and provide an atmosphere that encourages open dialogue.

- Belcan does good work and expects a fair price for our services.

- Belcan is a company that cares for its employees and clients.

- Listen to the customer. The customer comes first.

- Live by your word.

- With a positive attitude we will meet our goals, if we don't care who gets credit.

- If you make a mistake, admit it; if you don't know, say you don't know.

- Think positive about your work and life.

"Ruth was the manager, organized and detail oriented," Massie observed in a book about the Andersons. "Ralph was the entrepreneur, dreaming and taking chances."

After incorporation was complete, Ralph began the process of seeking customers. He had plenty of knowledge and contacts, but progress was slow. During the first three years of its existence, Belcan Corporation cleared about $200. Nothing auspicious, but like those orphan lambs, it helped lay a foundation for the future.

Entering the Age of Robotics

In 1976 George Lucas changed the film industry with the introduction of the Star Wars movie. Kenner Toys had secured the rights to produce all of the film's merchandise. Kenner in turn, contracted with Belcan to produce a working model of R2D2 to be used in a TV commercial. The working model was constructed from a drawing supplied by Twentieth Century Films.

MO-GARD

FOOT PROTECTOR

BELCAN CORP. 9505 MONTGOMERY RD.

CINCINNATI 42, OHIO

Fig. 2

Fig. 5

Fig. 3

INVENTOR.
RALPH G. ANDERSON
HAROLD S. SHARP

BY

Tritle & Schenk

height keeps feet from blade

special non-skid cleats

Warni

Lawn Mower Safety
Up to Individual Now

Foot Cut
By Mower

KEOSAUQUA

Foot Cut by

The Early Years:
Determination Conquers a Tough Business Climate

While the recent track record of Belcan Corporation appears glorious, the business climate in 1958 offered few guarantees. The failure rate for new businesses in the United States loomed at fifty-six percent the year that an enthusiastic young couple set up shop in a one-room office on the second floor of a Cincinnati building.

Ralph and Ruth Anderson were not blind to the cold reality of the business world, but they countered it with a warm determination. Ralph arranged appointments and looked for customers.

Ruth answered the phone and kept the books. For them, success – and the potential for failure – were highly personal matters.

It was, indeed, the 1950s. Ruth and Ralph watched on a black and white television as evening news anchors Chet Huntley and David Brinkley reported that the nuclear-powered submarine USS Nautilus had become the first vessel to cross the North Pole underwater. They heard about President Eisenhower signing an

act accepting Alaska as the forty-ninth state. It was an era that would see the Soviet Union launch Sputnik 3 and Elvis Presley enter the U.S. Army.

Ralph and Ruth were not blind
to the cold reality of the business world,
but they countered it
with a warm determination.

Story of the Mo-Gard

Ralph G. Anderson's entrepreneurial nature led to his first patent, which was for Mo-Gard, a plastic device that could protect the foot from sliding under a lawn mower. After placing 10,000 of the devices in retail outlets, Belcan's CEO began to have second thoughts. "I got a little uneasy about having the liability of people getting their foot cut off and suing me, so I took all 10,000 of them to the dump." Ralph says of the experience, "I learned that it's wise to stick to what you know."

Building a Team

From the very beginning, Ralph G. Anderson chose his team carefully, although he also vowed that he could gain a fairly good assessment of a person at a first encounter. "If you see somebody in person, you can read them," he explains. "I think there is a lot to that."

By slowly and steadily building a list of acquaintances in the business world, especially in engineering, Ralph developed ready access to some of his best team members.

"You have to get the best people," he says, "and be honest with them. I'm not a big shot, and I don't want a big shot working for me. Every person has to be in the right slot. You can't push people, you have to lead them." Ralph easily sums up his approach to personnel matters: "I am a people person, and I believe you have to be honest, trust the people around you, and have faith in them."

Ralph defines management as people. He contends that the philosophy did not come from

(continued on page 31)

"I am a people person, and I believe you have to be honest, trust the people around you, and have faith in them."

-Ralph G. Anderson

GIESEL ENGINE MODEL
U.S. ARMY
TANK AUTOMOTIVE COMMAND

.belcan.
CORPORATION

books; it's a matter of common sense. Only after the company began to grow did he add a director of human resources. For many years, he and Ruth served in that capacity.

The teamwork approach is a core principle at Belcan; not simply an industry buzzword, but the only method of conducting business practiced

> The teamwork approach
> is a core principle
> at Belcan;
> not simply a buzzword,
> but the only method
> of conducting business.

by the company. The engineers typically work together in project teams, but the corporate management group at Belcan operates as a lean, agile team without specific corporate quotas. The entire group is responsible for the team's actions. "Working without quotas is hard for some people," says Executive Assistant Vicki Jenkins. "A few who have left the company may have needed more structure."

Ralph G. Anderson cites one particular example of teamwork. "We bid on a rig for a large customer, so we sat down and talked about it. In a situation like that, if it doesn't work, we're a team. We don't have to meet goals every quarter. That's a healthy approach, but if you worry about it, it's not." There is no designated sales staff at Belcan because Ralph believes that every employee is a salesperson. Quoting one

of his favorite motivational mentors, Wayne Dyer, Ralph observes that it's important "to fall in love with your work, and sell the love."

In the early days of Belcan, as Ralph prepared to launch a technical services division (placing professional engineers with companies to complete specialty projects), he employed a unique strategy to recruit employees.

"I went down to Florida, where a Pratt-Whitney facility was laying off engineers, and checked into a motel. Engineers heard I was there and started coming over for interviews. I told them what I could pay and signed them up as fast as I could. I found nearly 200 people for our project."

Ralph believes that every employee is a salesperson.

Story of the Geisel

In 1969, Jack Hope, Vice President of Cummins Engine, mentioned to Ralph Anderson that Cummins needed an engine. Working with Robert Johnston, the team developed the Geisel, a revolutionary turbo-charged diesel engine. Jack Hope left Cummins and the pair formed HAECO, Hope Anderson Engine Company, and acquired a patent for the Geisel engine in the late 1970s.

Ralph Anderson describes the engine as a gas turbine and a diesel put together. "Take a little compressor and pump air into the diesel at a 4-to-1 compression ratio, don't cool it, and run it up to 1700° F air. You double the horsepower and cut fuel consumption by 40 percent." The Army was interested in the Giesel because 60 percent of the maintenance on a tank engine is the cooling system. The Giesel requires no water cooling.

"The charter on Mr. Anderson's desk impressed me. He really runs the company that way."

"Belcan has always been at least twenty years ahead of the curve in many ways. It is a forward-thinking company, always looking for new opportunities."

"Belcan doesn't *have* a product. We *design* products for our customers."

"We emphasize selling what the customers want."

"Mr. Anderson continually emphasizes working as a team."

"This company has a family culture. The chain of command is short and focused on joint buy-in."

"Unlike public companies, we don't shoot people who make mistakes."

Teamwork Is Belcan's Greatest Asset
Comments from the Team

"Belcan is committed to excellence, dedicated to the customer and customer service and respect for the individual. Belcan's greatest assets are its people."

- from the Belcan Charter

"Belcan fully embraces technology. When I joined the company, they were way ahead of the curve in computer-aided design. I accepted a position on the spot."

"The neat thing is you don't have all those layers of management. It's more of a teamwork environment. Keeps us very nimble and agile."

"This company's product mix is why it's where it is now. We've survived the ebb and flow of engineering, technical, and staffing."

"Belcan is a quiet company with high values that filter down."

Belcan in Action with Procter & Gamble:
Quality Improvement (QI) Program - The Pampers Project

The vast scope of Belcan and its capacity for responding to clients became fully evident in 1983 when Procter & Gamble offered the company one of its greatest challenges. There was an unlikely focus for this tremendous feat of engineering: disposable diapers.

By November of 1983, American families had become accustomed to the convenience of disposable diapers, but few were aware of the fierce competition that existed behind the scenes among companies producing the various brands. Procter and Gamble had perfected a disposable diaper in 1961. In the 1980s, Kimberly Clark entered the business and grabbed a big share of the market with Huggies.

Procter & Gamble, known for an aggressive sense of competition, decided to respond with a reconfiguration of its products that would require the design of new machines in all of its plants. Competitive pressure dictated that the

> Few families were aware
> of the fierce competition
> that existed among
> companies producing
> various brands of diapers.

new machines be designed in minimum time. Belcan was the company with the expertise to meet this challenge.

The first stages for obtaining the huge design project began with the allocation of 15,000 square feet for a model shop in a new building on Kemper Road. Quickly, the space was expanded to 45,000 square feet and Belcan became committed to the largest single project in its history.

There was no time to sequence the design steps in normal order. Initial drawings would take too long; therefore, the project moved to the construction of full scale plastic and wood models built for multiple machine lines in four Procter & Gamble plants. Belcan would then contract out for the production of the metal parts as drawings were produced.

> There was no time
> to sequence the design steps
> in normal order. Initial
> drawings would take
> too long. The project moved to the
> construction of wooden models.

Memories of an Ambitious Undertaking

Ralph G. Anderson has vivid memories of the particular challenges inherent in the Pampers contract. "In 1983," he recalls, "Procter & Gamble came to us to discuss a very large project. We knew we could do it, but to make it work, Belcan had to hire people and make it possible for them to meet the deadlines." Belcan ended up renting houses and cars for project workers.

"P&G's major requirement was that we meet their schedules. We managed to do that with eleven plants in seven countries. We went up to 275 people, then 400. We had to take over some of the vendor shops. The first production line was up and running in the first plant in only seven months after we started the project."

Little wonder that Ralph takes special pride in that contract work. "We did what we said we would do ... one of the biggest and best jobs we've put out. P&G said it was a miracle we got the job done."

The success of the project depended upon rapid response between the trials of the full scale models and the revised orders for the metal parts. As the models indicated needed changes, the orders were issued for updates. Even though this process resulted in extra costs, the entire project was schedule-driven. Target dates had to be met if the project was to be successful.

The Pampers project required competent engineers who would not hesitate to make changes in the routine patterns learned in school.

> The Pampers project required
> competent engineers
> who would not hesitate
> to make changes in the routine
> patterns learned in school.

Additionally, management required a rapid communications system and cooperation among professional personnel. The flexibility that was a major characteristic of Ralph Anderson and his small, young firm made it possible to operate a tight ship with numerous components.

At one time, the strain on space became so great that a new 45,000 square foot Kemper Road building, which had been planned for operations, was utilized solely for storing parts to be shipped to the customer's plants. In another instance, Belcan assumed control of the operation of the subcontractor in order to meet the aggressive schedule.

During the period from 1984-1985, the Pampers project required a major effort by most of Belcan's employees. Ultimately, the company hit every time target that had been set; the machines had been installed in the P&G plants enabling the company to regain a major portion of the disposable diaper market.

The Wisdom of Anderson

Even in the midst of its most intense and demanding activities, such as the Pampers Project, Belcan has enjoyed a high degree of employee loyalty. As Ralph G. Anderson notes with pride: "Our in-house engineering operation is very stable; there is very little turnover. Some employees have been with Belcan for over forty years."

The reason, as many Belcan employees would explain, is that the CEO himself shows great faith in other people and gives them ample opportunity to use their skills and knowledge. Experts might call it a personnel policy. Ralph says it's common sense.

At a Glance: QI Program

- 1000 design releases
- 2000 engineering instructions to the plants
- 5000 drawings
- 4000 purchase orders for 600 million dollars of equipment
- Peak staff level of 400 workers
- Production line up and running after only seven months

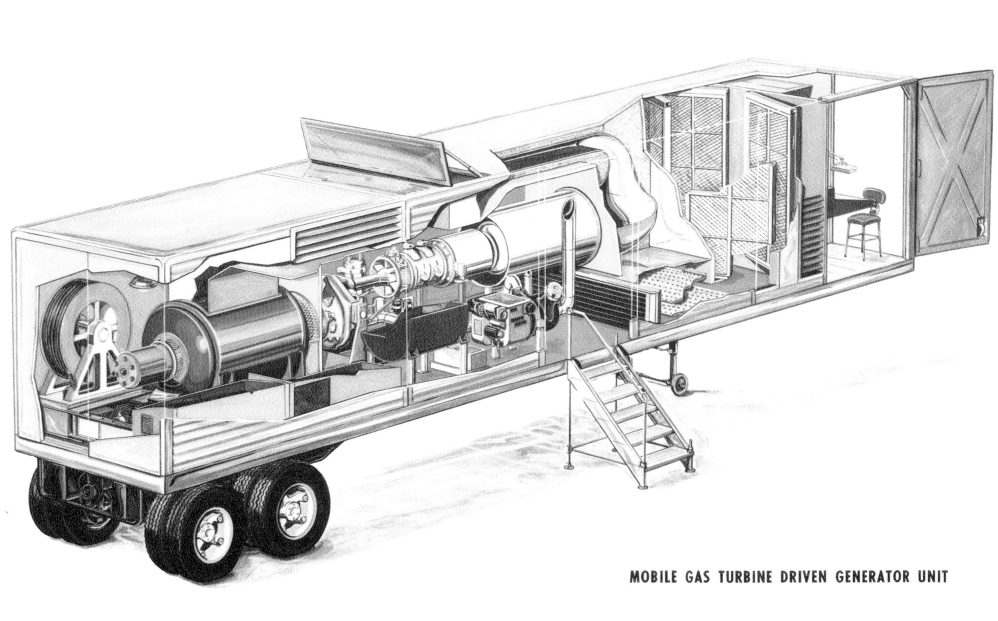

MOBILE GAS TURBINE DRIVEN GENERATOR UNIT

In personnel interviews, Ralph takes an intuitive approach. "My feeling is I can determine in the first ten minutes whether a person is qualified. I don't have a rating system. It's a matter of personality and gut feelings."

Ralph's system apparently is effective. Belcan has a reputation for attracting and retaining key personnel. The Belcan CEO takes pride in the fact that many of the firm's employees have remained loyal through decades of work.

From the Pen to the Computer

As a young engineer with a fresh degree, Ralph G. Anderson called on acquaintances and companies in search of engineering jobs. During this early period, Ralph Anderson earned a reputation as an excellent engineer in the field of testing stress in aircraft engines.

Engineering problems in the 1950s and 60s were solved by applying analytical equations and formulas. Engineers often filled page after page with neatly hand-drafted analyses. In 1954, Ralph Anderson completed this example (photo at right): an application of Strain Energy Theory Analysis of a YJ67 Curtiss-Wright engine frame involving statics, stress, and differential equations.

Although the Belcan CEO was gifted with the ability to solve complex problems, his company became one of the first to embrace computer technology. Belcan purchased its first WANG computer in 1966 and added CALMA in 1980.

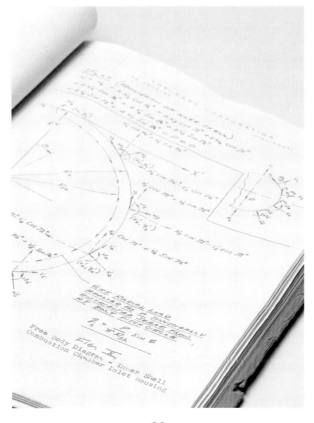

Turbine Power Systems, Inc. (TPS)

Consistent with his visionary and collaborative philosophy, Ralph G. Anderson entered into an ambitious contract with General Motors Overseas Division in 1974 to design and build portable, gas turbine-driven power generator units for underdeveloped nations (pictured on page 38). Anderson's new company, Turbine Power Systems, Inc., a grass-roots start-up operation, designed and produced the unit's base structure, exhaust collector, fuel, ventilation systems, and electrical control panels at the newly purchased Maineville, Ohio, Big Four Building (shown below). General Motors supplied the trucks and the Allison 501K engine. Three units were shipped to remote villages in Iraq and 14 to Egypt. Additionally, TPS personnel trained foreign technicians to operate and maintain the 3-megawatt systems.

Roger Penske purchased TPS in 1980 and renamed it Penske Power. The company, Rolls-Royce Energy Systems, Inc., is now located in Columbus, Ohio.

GE Aviation

The success of Belcan Corporation has come, for the most part, in steady growth and incremental steps forward. However, a few contracts and projects hold a special place in company history in terms of their size and scope, as well as the degree of challenge offered to the Belcan team. One such project involved an assignment from GE Aviation.

Late in 2006, Belcan employees gathered for the official signing of an infrastructure contract with GE Aviation that brought Belcan one of the largest projects in company history.

This new and ambitious project actually had its roots in one of Ralph G. Anderson's first engineering jobs. As a young man, he worked at a GE Aviation facility in Evendale, OH, and after that maintained a long history of professional associations and business alliances with the corporation. Even so, back when the young engineer was analyzing gas turbine aircraft engines, little did he realize that he would found an engineering firm that would maintain longterm associations with the giant corporation.

During the past decade, the number of collaborative global projects involving GE Aviation and Belcan has increased significantly. AETD President Phil Combs has developed relationships with key employees at the largest companies in the aviation industry, greatly enhancing Belcan's growth and stability.

On December 8, 2006, Belcan employees gathered to sign a contract for one of the largest projects in Belcan history. This ambitious project actually had its roots in one of Ralph G. Anderson's first engineering jobs. As a young man, he worked at a GE facility in Evendale, Ohio, and maintained professional contact with the corporation for years to come.

Photo left: Adding to Belcan's strong relationship with GE Aviation, in December, 2006, Ralph G. Anderson signed a five-year Infrastructure 'Super Center' contract with GE Aviation, expanding support to GE's Energy, Oil and Gas, Transportation, and Water divisions.

A Sampling of Belcan Customers

Across the years, Belcan has provided Engineering, TechServices, and product support for some of the world's most complex and widely respected businesses. A sampling of past and present customers would include:

Caterpillar
GE Aviation
DuPont
Honeywell
Rolls-Royce
Procter & Gamble
Pratt & Whitney
GE Lighting Systems

The Wisdom of Anderson

When Belcan was a small company, Ralph G. Anderson practiced what he termed 'management by wandering around.' Each day, he arrived early, stayed late, and moved among the various offices to observe what was going on in the company.

Now that Belcan has 8,000 employees around the world, Ralph uses modern technology to communicate. Employees and friends of Belcan find a motivational quote from Ralph in their email inbox at 8:30 a.m. each day. With technical assistance from Vicki Jenkins, Ralph chooses a quote, motto, or saying that is thought provoking but always positive.

Belcan Telecommunications Manager Jane Gilliam notes the CEO's ability to brighten her day. "His motivational message for the day is always exactly what I need," she says.

UNITED STATES

Grand Rapi

Chicago -

Peoria ---

Provo ---

Phoenix ---

Dallas ---

Austin ---

CHINA

Shanghai

Dayton
Detroit
Mt. Vernon
Cleveland
Lynn
Windsor Locks
East Hartford
Simsbury
Wethersfield
Stratford
Pittsburgh
Baltimore
Gaithersburg
Charleston
Lynchburg
Smithfield
Raleigh
Cary
Charlotte
Cincinnati
Fairfield / Hamilton / Milford
Florence
Greenville
Lexington
West Palm
Atlanta
Indianapolis
St. Louis
ytown
ston

UNITED KINGDOM

Doncaster
Bristol

Going Global:
Belcan Extends Its Reach

Across the fifty years of its existence, Belcan has remained nimble and profitable by constantly adapting to new realities in the competitive world of business. If a customer in Indianapolis needs help with a sizeable and complex engineering project, Belcan is willing to open a TechServices office in Indianapolis. If the worldwide business climate reflects growing opportunities in Europe, Belcan is prepared to open offices in England.

The ability to adapt has given Belcan a presence in locations ranging from Raleigh, North Carolina, to Phoenix, Arizona, and more recently, in England and China. But regardless of the time zone or the size and shape of the building, the business emphasis has remained constant: excel in serving your customers.

Belcan has remained
nimble and profitable
by constantly adapting
to new realities
in the competitive
world of business

How Belcan Serves Its Customers:
Solutions, Services, Technology

Belcan Corporation has a number of divisions that seek to meet particular needs of varied clients at locations around the world.

Staffing Solutions
This division recruits and employs individuals in the clerical, professional and light industrial markets. Belcan's Professional Search Specialists work diligently to find the perfect staff for clients' direct-hire positions. This enables clients to eliminate the dollars and hours invested in advertising, searching on the Internet, interviewing, testing, and screening potential employees

TechServices
This segment of Belcan recruits and employs a wide range of technical professionals to augment clients' workforces throughout the United States and abroad.

Specialized Services
Belcan offers software sales, technical support, training, and mentoring.

Information Technology
IT specialists provide businesses with enterprise solutions for business and staffing support. These fields include Enterprise Consulting, System Integration, Network and Telephony, Data Services, and Staffing Support Solutions.

Multimedia Services

The Multimedia Services unit develops training that is delivered online or from a computer station and can create a trade show booth, a projected presentation, or a series of printed brochures. Services include Video Production, eLearning, Interactive Media, 2D and 3D Graphics, and Presentation Design and Print Media.

Belcan Engineering

Engineering services are offered worldwide, with a specialization in design engineering, engineering analysis, computer modeling, and advanced manufacturing techniques. Here are some specific types of engineering services:

- Conceptual & Product Design Engineering
- Full Design / Drafting Capability
- Product Improvement
- Controls Software & Hardware
- Cost / Weight Reduction
- Field Failure Assessment / Correction
- Heat Transfer & CFD
- Rapid Prototyping / SLA
- Tools, Fixtures Design & Manufacturing
- Hardware Procurement
- Material and Process Engineering
- Product Assurance
- Component Test Rig Design / Fabrication
- Instrumentation Design / Application
- Quality Assurance / Reliability Engineering
- Specialty Equipment Design & Build
- Stress & Vibration Analysis
- Technical Publications
- Test Support, Data Reduction, Reporting
- Testing: Cell, Wind Tunnel, Outdoor Acoustic, Operability, Performance

The Wisdom of Anderson

Despite the steady expansion of its offices and projects around the globe, Belcan has maintained a reputation for excellence in customer service. Ralph G. Anderson says that is possible only because Belcan makes it a high priority to find and hire the most dependable, hard-working people to join its team.

Ralph has invested a great deal of time and energy in this process, yet he makes it sound utterly simple: "We find good people through relationships established over the years, through listening." And when he personally is conducting an interview, he doesn't hesitate to rely on gut feelings:

"My final decision is made by intuition." In case that sounds too casual, Ralph adds a postscript: "I hire the best!"

45

Belcan Corporation:
A Timeline of Success

Belcan Corporation has never hesitated to provide better service by opening engineering and TechServices offices in any location essential to the needs of its customers. As a result, the company timeline features an eclectic mix of accomplishments in engineering, productivity, and adaptation, along with a healthy dose of office openings. Every change has represented the company's determination to serve its customers.

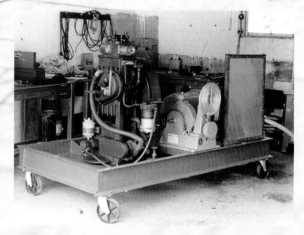

1958-62

• Belcan Corporation founded; first office located at 9505 Montgomery Road in Montgomery, OH (1958)

• Mo-Gard patent issued (1960)

• Indiana Gear becomes first project to generate corporate income (1962)

1963-66

• Mr. Anderson leads Allstate's Indianapolis office for Allison (1963)

• Belcan opens Indianapolis engineering office for Allison (1966)

1967-69

• Office moves to new location in Montgomery, OH (1967)

• Pratt & Whitney on-site program begins in West Palm Beach, FL (1969)

• Design of single cylinder test Engine Systems - HAECO (1969)

1960s: Good News for the Number Crunchers Belcan made a daring move in 1966 while operating an Engineering facility for General Motors. The firm installed desk-top electronic calculators capable of computing logarithms. Suddenly engineers were no longer dependent on mechanical calculators, and Belcan had entered the computer age.

Belcan: A Timeline of Success

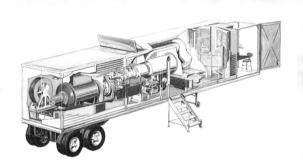

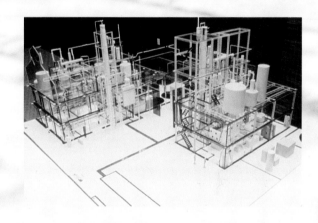

1970-71

- GE Aviation tooling design work begins in Montgomery Road office (1970)

- Test of single-cylinder Test Engine Systems (1970)

- Pratt & Whitney on-site program completed in West Palm Beach, FL (1971)

1972

- Started design of Industrial Turbine Packages for GMOS (1972)

- Turbine Power Systems unit formed to design and build turbine generating packages for GMOS; moved to new facility in Maineville, OH (1974)

1976

- Deerfield Road building opens

- Engineering & TechServices are formed as separate divisions

- St. Louis TechServices office opens

1977

- Model Shop established

- Turbine Power Systems unit is purchased by Penske Power Systems

1970s: Teamwork in Blue Ash Ralph G. Anderson teamed up with Charles Kubicki in 1979 to establish the Blue Ash Industrial Center in the greater Cincinnati area. The park, which spanned 130 acres, began with a building known as Kemper East and later grew to include the Goldcoast Building, which was home to Belcan TechServices.

Belcan: A Timeline of Success

1978

• Opened TechServices office in Phoenix with some engineering services

• Acquired Wilde & Krause Architects

• Opened engineering operation in St. Louis, MO

• Leased Junior Achievement building on Ashfield Drive in Blue Ash, OH

1979

• Formed partnership with CUC and started Blue Ash Industrial Center.

• Opened TechServices office in Charlotte, NC

1980

• Anderson Way building opened

• First engineering computer system (CALMA) adopted by Belcan

1981-82

• Opened TechServices office in Indianapolis, IN (1981)

• Opened TechServices office in Los Angeles (1981)

• Introduced media services for product support (1981)

• Opened TechServices office in New Orleans, LA (1982)

1980s: Evolving Design-Build In 1987, the Lodge and Shipley Machine Tool Company (owned by the Manuflex Divison of Belcan) found a way to help GE Aviation improve its component manufacturing system. LS built fully automated turning cells featuring digital technology for constant feedback and quality control. Performance exceeded expectations, with throughput more than doubled over the previous system.

Belcan: A Timeline of Success

1982-83

- Kemper East & West buildings opened (1982)
- Opened TechServices office in Charleston, WV (1982)
- Procter & Gamble QI Program started (1983)
- Model Shop moved to Kemper East (1983)
- TechServices moved headquarters to new Kemper East building (1983)

1984

- DuPont REOP begins in Pittsburgh
- Northlake building opens
- Opened TechServices offices in Richmond, Atlanta, San Francisco, Dallas, Glendale (CA), Houston, and Austin

1985

- Opened TechServices offices in Raleigh, Nashville, and Tucson
- Purchased Multicon
- Construction division formed
- TechServices moved headquarters to new GoldCoast building

1986

- Anderson Way building expansion
- Engineering operation started in Indianapolis for Allison
- BGP formed
- Northland Building purchased
- TechServices office opens in Cleveland, OH

Belcan: A Timeline of Success

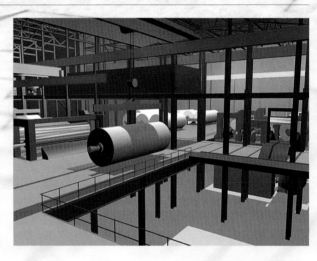

1987

- TechServices office opens in Long Beach

- Ulticon is formed

- Purchased Lodge & Shipley

- Advanced Manufacturing Technology begins in Cleveland

- SEED starts in Solon, OH

- Daytona Center for Automotive Testing put in operation in Dayton

1989

- TechServices offices open in Charleston, WV, and Pittsburgh

- Established partnering relationship with Eli Lilly

- TechServices moves to their own accounting system

- GE Aviation Blanket Purchase Order started

1991

- GE Aviation Alliance started

- Purchased the BGP partners for sole ownership

1992

- Mead Engineering project started

- Incorporated Belcan Business Temporaries

- Acquired McGraw Eng. & Design, Inc. in Middletown, OH, and Ashland, KY

- Formed CSA (Custodio Suarez & Assoc.) in Puerto Rico

1990s: No Headaches for Bayer In 1994, Belcan won a multi-year contract with the Bayer Corporation to provide on-site engineering and design services. A full complement of engineering and design services were performed on mechanical equipment, piping systems, HVAC, and controls, and as well as civil, structural and electrical instrumentation.

Belcan: A Timeline of Success

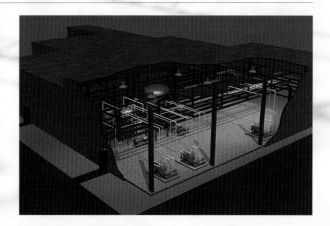

1993

• JD Edwards computer system starts

• GE Carbondale Tooling Center purchased from General Electric

• Staffing Services purchases "Tri Temp" & "Select-A-Staff"

1995

• TechServices purchased PATSCO offices in Wilmington, DE, and Baton Rouge, LA

• Dyer-Belcan joint venture starts

1996

• Bayer Pittsburgh on-site partnership starts

• Purchased ATI in Mobile and Houston

• Opened Phoenix Engineering Office - Honeywell

On the Move in the New Millenium In 2003, Belcan began a strategic planning process aimed at expanding the firm's global reach. One result was the opening of an engineering center in Shanghai, China. The center provides design and analysis support for Belcan's U.S. customers in the aerospace, automotive, heavy equipment, and consumer product industries.

Belcan: A Timeline of Success

1997-98

- Opened Lynn Engineering office - GE Aviation (1997)

- Opened West Palm Beach office for Pratt & Whitney (1998)

- Purchased ATC in Bristol and Derby, England (1998)

- Created staffing franchise (1998)

1999-2000

- Opened TechServices office in Tulsa, OK (1999)

- Access Personnel purchased by Staffing Services (2000)

- Opened Lexington, KY, Staffing Office (2000)

2001

- Took over Lockheed program in Gaithersburg, MD

- Purchased Dependable Data in London, KY, and former PVDNet

- Hamilton Sundstrand operation starts on-site

- Purchased AAC in Chicago, Peoria, and Ann Arbor

- Purchased Engineers USA in Cary, NC

- Opened Engineering office in Ann Arbor, MI

2002

- Opened Milford Engineering office - Sikorsky

- Opened Windsor Locks East Hartford Engineering office, Hamilton Sundstrand

- Opened Peoria Engineering office - Caterpillar

- UT500 Contract

- Started development of Virtual Medical Network (VMN)

Belcan: A Timeline of Success

2003

- Opened Cary, NC, Engineering office - Caterpillar
- Opened Engineering office in China
- Belcan Blanket Agreement with GE Aviation to serve seven engineering centers as sole source
- Opened TechServices office in East Hartford, CT

2004

- GE Aviation awards Belcan PDE Contract (Product Definition Engineering)
- Opened TechServices ATC office in Doncaster, England

2005

- Opened Lexington Engineering office - Sikorsky
- Opened Seattle Engineering office - Northrop
- Opened Middle River Aircraft Systems office - Baltimore, MD
- Leased PVDNet software rights
- Contracted operating interest in VMN
- Opened Cleveland Staffing office

2006-2008

- Belcan completes multi-axis transient thrust measurement test stand – Site 7, GE Aviation Peeble's Test Operations
- Opened Low Cost Center in Lexington, KY (2006)
- Belcan broadens its core business into different markets (2007)
- Belcan celebrates its 50th Anniversary (2008)

Farmers are good people. They know what hard work is, and they aren't afraid of it.

Ralph G. Anderson

ANDERSON CIRCLE FARM

Anderson Circle Farm

Agricultural heritage thrives in the heart of the bluegrass

Visitors to Anderson Circle Farm near Harrodsburg, Kentucky, are quick to encounter the Farm's imposing stone gateway and a green-roofed complex known as the Sale Barn. Above the immaculately-kept grounds and facilities three flags wave in the breeze, showing the colors of the United States, the Commonwealth of Kentucky, and Anderson Circle.

Those colors crown a picturesque summit that affords a panoramic view of the surrounding countryside. Anderson Circle Farm stretches as far as the eye can see. Ralph G. Anderson grew up on Warwick Road, just outside Harrodsburg, and Anderson Circle Farm is located on both sides of Warwick Road.

The process of acquiring land for the farm began with a discussion between Ralph and Ruth Anderson. "In the mid-1960s, my wife and I would always get into discussions at tax time. I thought, I'll just buy a farm and commit the money, and we'll make the payments and know where the money went. It's teamwork." Investing in the land appeared to be a good strategy to both the Andersons.

In October of 1967, the Andersons purchased their first 220 acres, known as the Bissett Farm, on Curry Road for $350 per acre. Fifteen years later, raw land with no water and no buildings commanded $5,000 per acre. Today, Central Kentucky land values have soared.

The process for acquiring farmland began in 1967 with a discussion between Ralph and Ruth.

As the appraised value of the farm multiplied, so did additional purchases. The names of Ballard, Wilkinson, Chapline, Kennedy, Balden, and thirty other farms have been deeded under the Anderson Circle name. (Kentucky farms are often named for an early owner or in some cases, for the immediate past one.) The Anderson Circle farm now encompasses 7,000 acres, 120 miles of black plank fencing, 12 miles of paved roads, 15 houses, 85 barns, and 3,000 head of cattle. In years past, the barns and fields have been home to other crops and animals, but black Angus cattle have always grazed on the verdant pastures.

Central Kentucky's Maury silt loam soil is considered to be the finest nature provides for raising crops including hay, corn, tobacco, wheat, and vegetables. Typical of Anderson Circle Farm land, well drained and teeming with good organisms, the fertile soil is highly desired. Mother Nature controls the farmer's plans, and, as have most farms, Anderson Circle has endured blizzards, hailstorms, floods, and several long, parching droughts. But as evidence of the enduring quality of the land and those who love it, spring brings regeneration of growth, and the cycle begins again.

Utilizing modern technology, much of it developed by Belcan Corporation, Anderson Circle uses labor, maintenance, and inventory-tracking software. The entire acreage has been mapped to indicate every building, road, gate, fence, utility line, and meter. All are recorded and coded for data management purposes. Information is utilized with a handheld computer module to track repairs and maintenance. Over the years the farm has demonstrated cutting-edge farming practices, including a double-batch tobacco barn, silos, and mechanical continuous feed handlers, manure liquefying for compost, and other technology-driven agricultural practices.

Every Anderson Circle animal is identified with modern electronic identification tags. Chute-side computers and radio-frequency identification maintain records on animal weight and health. The

In October of 1967, the Andersons purchased their first 220 acres known as the Bissett Farm on Curry Road for $350 per acre. Fifteen years later, raw land with no water and no buildings commanded $5,000 per acre. Today, Central Kentucky land values have soared.

commercial herd is coupled with a purebred Angus program, in which cattle have known genetic qualities and ratings, including DNA history.

Each time a new parcel of land was acquired, Ralph G. Anderson and his farm team developed a plan for the ultimate integrated farm. Soon after the sale closed on a new farm, black fencing was constructed. Entrances to all primary Anderson Circle Farm facilities are flanked with Kentucky stone fences and wrought iron gates. Additionally, natural areas are respected by maintaining native flora and fauna, including woodlands and habitat that protect turkey and deer.

The farm rotates crops as a conservation practice, has a policy of limited chemical usage, and uses no-till practices to control soil erosion. Anderson Circle Farm maintains its philosophy of respecting and cooperating with nature's provisions.

The entire acreage has been mapped to indicate every building, road, gate, fence, utility line, and meter. All are recorded and coded for data management purposes.

Anderson Circle Farm Show and Sale Barn

With the Show Barn as headquarters, Anderson Circle Farm maintains high visibility on U.S. 127 close to Harrodsburg. In 1987, the Anderson Circle complex began to grow and was gaining national recognition for its cattle program. Ralph G. Anderson brought the team together and began the process of designing and building a 14,500 square-foot complex of barns, sales arena and adjoining cattle pens, meeting facilities, and farm office.

The chief Belcan architect, Isaac Gilliam, recalls Ralph requesting that the barn be a strong visual statement reflecting the long and proud tradition of Kentucky farming. Utilizing the iconic symbols of the American barn, including irregular roof lines, gable ends, and the ubiquitous cupola, the cedar and limestone structure is capped by a standing seam metal roof.

Respecting design elements from Kentucky horse and tobacco barns, the Anderson Circle team created a new generation cattle barn, complete with a modern, fully-equipped laboratory.

The barn's open spacious lobby, supported by a fully-equipped commercial kitchen, accommodates several hundred guests. The Andersons are avid supporters of the arts and have commissioned original works including sculptures and paintings. As an added design element, bronze reproductions of Frederick Remington sculptures grace the entrance.

Respecting design elements from
Kentucky horse and tobacco
barns, the Anderson
Circle team created
a new generation cattle barn,
complete with a modern,
fully-equipped laboratory.

Anderson Circle Farm maintains a philosophy of respecting and cooperating with nature's provisions.

Ralph G. Anderson

Anderson Circle Farm is home to 3,000 head of cattle and also serves as a site for social events as well as cattle sales. Belcan architect Isaac Gilliam (left, with Ralph G. Anderson) played a key role in planning new structures and renovating historic buildings at Anderson Circle.

Continuing his support of education, Ralph Anderson makes his Anderson Circle Farm available to community and civic groups for meetings and educational seminars. Clubs such as 4-H and FFA visit to learn about the operation of a farm

In addition to being one of the largest working farms in Kentucky, Anderson Circle Farm has become a tourist attraction, drawing busloads of visitors each year.

Incorporating a state-of-the art sales ring and arena, the Anderson Circle Barn has hosted some of the premier purebred Angus sales in the country. Buyers from 45 states have visited the Mercer County area for shows and sales.

Black Angus cattle have always grazed on Anderson Circle Farm pastures.

Ralph G. Anderson

Ralph G. Anderson has commissioned several works by Crittenden, Ky., woodcarver David J. Monhollen, including this circular walnut relief sculpture featuring prominent buildings and other landmarks from Anderson Circle Farm.

A Farm Unlike Any Other:
Historic Preservation at Anderson Circle

The late Thomas Clark, Kentucky's Historian Laureate and longtime chair of the history department at the University of Kentucky, delighted in visiting with Ralph G. Anderson. Dr. Clark and his wife Loretta especially enjoyed a tour of Ralph and Ruth's elegant Walnut Hall mansion and Anderson Circle Farm. One hot summer afternoon in 1998 as the farm hosted a cattle production sale, Dr. Clark, a farmer himself, expressed amazement as Anderson Circle Farm's prized purebred Angus stock paraded through the handsome sales ring and commanded industry-topping prices.

Dr. Clark and Ralph Anderson shared a love of history and a life-long commitment to historic preservation. Over the years, Ralph has saved and restored the historic homes and cemeteries that existed on farms he purchased.

During the 1990s, Ralph and Ruth authorized extensive archaeological excavations to be conducted on their land by the University of Kentucky. Findings of that study have added greatly to the understanding of Mercer County's role in Kentucky history. Mercer County was the first region in Kentucky to be settled by frontiersmen from the colonies, and many historic sites remain in good condition, dating back over 200 years.

The concept of a "station" was important during frontier days, referring to a residential structure designed for defense and protection during Indian attacks. The boundaries of Anderson Circle Farm encompass four such historic sites, including McGary's Station and Ray's Station.

Anderson Circle Farm has grown through the purchase of more than thirty-four individual farms since 1967. Teams of dedicated individuals from the farm and Belcan Corporation have made a concerted effort to preserve and protect facilities and land. Many historic cemeteries and graveyards were discovered on the various farms. At least six have been preserved and improved through a series of steps that includes cleaning, repairing, and securing each headstone, followed by the construction of fences for further protection. In the words of Ralph Anderson, "It is important to Anderson Circle Farm and its employees that we preserve the past and honor and respect those who traveled this way."

To assemble an expert team, Ralph G. Anderson called on gifted architects, engineers, and designers. Isaac Gilliam, Belcan's Vice President of Facilities and Information Technology, has served as chief architect for restoration and construction. Cincinnati designer David Millet selected the furnishings, draperies, and artwork for the houses. Jerry and Paul Wilson, owners of Wilson Brothers Construction Company of Harrodsburg, have provided many of the skilled craftsmen required to bring the historic structures to new life.

> Ralph and Ruth authorized extensive archaeological excavations. The findings added greatly to the understanding of Mercer County's role in Kentucky history.

Walnut Hall: An Epic Restoration Project

Walnut Hall, an elegant Greek revival mansion, has been a landmark in Mercer County for over 150 years. Ralph G. Anderson has fond memories of the house from his childhood days in nearby Harrodsburg.

The story of the house began in 1840 when David W. Thompson began laying the stone foundation after locating local sources of limestone and clay. Construction continued for four years, producing a home that was a handsome showplace. The 8,000 square-foot mansion featured first and second-floor rooms with fourteen-foot ceilings, twelve working fireplaces, and floors made of poplar planks. Historical records documented the fact that the woodwork, doors, windows, and trim were milled from walnut trees grown on the farm. The fifteen-inch baseboards were constructed from seven pieces of walnut.

On the home's exterior, the main façade featured five bays. The central entrance was covered by a two-story pediment portico supported by four Ionic columns built with brick and covered with plaster.

By the time the Andersons acquired Walnut Hall in 1985 (as part of the purchase of the Gregory farm), the residence had suffered from

years of neglect. The house had no electricity or bathrooms, and much of the mansion had become a storage area for hay and grain.

> By 1985, the mansion
> had suffered years of neglect
> and was being used
> to store hay and grain.

After a two-year renovation, Walnut Hall was restored to its original state of grandeur and was named to the National Register of Historic Places. The mansion became the primary residence at Anderson Circle for Ralph and Ruth. Friends recall the couple's generosity in sharing Walnut Hall with the community at Christmas parties and charity events. Today, Ralph Anderson hosts an annual Belcan family picnic at the farm, welcoming employees for hayrides and good food.

The restoration team cleared, reseeded, and planted Walnut Hall's fourteen-acre lawn with many varieties of trees, creating a stately approach to the mansion. The rough gravel drive has been replaced with a tree-lined central

The Executive Committee of
the Gala Ball
cordially invites you to

Antebellum Revisited

to be held at
Mr. and Mrs. Ralph Anderson's
Walnut Hall
Saturday, the twelfth of September,
Nineteen hundred ninety-two,
for the benefit of
The Ragged Edge Theatre

Kevin Cole   Cocktails
                                              Hors d'oeuvres

                                              Black Tie
Dancing   (Post Civil War attire optional)
8:00-12:00

> "We would come down here
> to Walnut Hall,
> sit in each room
> and marvel at the
> workmanship."
> - *Ralph G. Anderson*

> "It's so welcoming.
> The place feels
> like home."
> - *Ruth Anderson,*
> *from a 1988 interview*

promenade culminating in a circular avenue for visitors.

The Andersons' grandchildren, Jason, Matthew, and Amanda McCaw, recall visiting the farm for family Thanksgiving celebrations. Per family tradition, the youngsters insisted on running the length of the Walnut Hall driveway from road to front porch, where they were greeted by their grandmother's hugs and the welcoming fragrance of a delicious Thanksgiving meal.

Other visitors have especially enjoyed Ruth Anderson's doll collection, which included U.S. Presidents' wives, baby dolls, and many more.

Abraham Chapline Plantation

Abraham Chapline Plantation: A Connection to Kentucky Frontiersmen

Chapline's descendents are buried in the cemetery that remains a part of the farm.

In 1774, before the American colonies had earned the right to be called an independent nation, the colonial government sent out explorers and surveyors to evaluate and lay claim to the area that was known as the land beyond the mountains. The region that some Indians called Kantucke was especially rich in game and fertile soil, and frontiersmen eagerly explored its hills and valleys.

One of those frontier explorers, James Harrod, reached the area that would become Mercer County in 1774, and his surveying party included a man named Abraham Chapline.

Chapline settled in the area and gradually accumulated a sizeable holding of 1,400 acres of land. His descendents later owned the land, and some are buried in the family cemetery that remains a part of the farm.

The Chapline mansion is one of the most imposing structures on the Anderson Circle Farm.

Over the years, the Chapline land changed owners and was divided into smaller parcels. One such portion became the 425-acre Rice Farm, purchased by Ralph G. Anderson in 2004.

The stately mansion that came with the parcel was not the home of Abraham Chapline, but the building now bears his name. It also has been known locally as the Rufus Henry VanArsdall House. Featuring late Queen Anne and Colonial Revival architectural style, flanked by Roman ionic columns, the Chapline House is one of the most imposing structures on the Anderson Circle Farm, and is currently utilized as a guest house.

Wildwood

Wildwood:
The William W. Goddard House

Wildwood, a high Victorian Italianate house completed in 1861, anchored the 400-acre Patterson Farm on Curry Pike at the time that Ralph and Ruth purchased the land. Now listed on the National Register of Historic Places, Wildwood was the second major restoration project undertaken by the Andersons.

This historic home derives its name from species of native trees collected and planted by the original owners, the Goddard family. Black locust, walnut, ash, tulip poplar, elm, and oak trees were planted in abundance on the eighteen-acre lawn, as well as hemlock, linden, willow, ash, and many other varieties.

After the Andersons purchased the Patterson property, their friends, the Dedmans, enjoyed recounting stories of the long and colorful history of the Goddards of Wildwood, who had a long association with the Dedman family.

A memorable book, *Uncle Will of Wildwood*, by Frances Jewell McVey and Robert Jewell, describes the unique characteristics of their uncle, Will Goddard, whose life spanned much of the 19th century. A financier, economist, and mechanic, Uncle Will was known for his fast pace, quick temper, and impulsive nature. On foot or horseback, Uncle Will used only one gait: a high run.

> This historic home derives its name from the many species of native trees collected and planted by the original owners, the Goddard family.

Wildwood produced a wealth of products, including greatly-admired saddle horses and shorthorn cattle. Will Goddard's neighbors were prosperous stock breeders and farmers, building considerable wealth by hemp, tobacco, and livestock production. During Uncle Will's lifetime, Mercer County was admired for the extremely fertile soil and abundant water supply, which made it possible to establish a thriving agricultural community.

The restoration of Wildwood did not prove to be as difficult as that of Walnut Hall, because the home had been continually inhabited over the years. The Anderson team added new electrical wiring and upgraded the heating and air conditioning system. The woodwork was stripped and refinished, the plaster repaired, and the floors refinished.

Wildwood was built on a t-shaped plan with a three-story tower and a one-story wraparound porch. Wood milled for construction was harvested from walnut, oak, and ash trees grown on the farm. The remains of a brick kiln were discovered in the yard, indicating that the original bricks were fired on site.

Wildwood served as the farm office and residence for Anderson Circle Farm's general manager before the Show Barn was constructed.

The Springhouse

The Springhouse:
New Life for an Old Structure

In 1988, the Andersons purchased a tract known as the Wilkinson Farm. An inspection of the property revealed that a barn, which appeared to be a typical five-bent tobacco barn, was actually a yellow poplar, mortise-and-tenon structure with joints connected by tapered pegs.

Such elements are typical of Shaker construction, and Ralph G. Anderson realized that the 100-year-old structure was too valuable from a historical standpoint to be a candidate for demolition. The decision was made to preserve the workmanship and materials.

Anderson Circle Farm was growing rapidly, and the Andersons needed a guesthouse. The poplar barn seemed perfectly suited to become a retreat and a haven for weekend getaways.

The Anderson Circle/Belcan restoration team carefully identified, tagged, and documented each piece of the structure. They subsequently reconstructed the Shaker barn on one of the most beautiful spots on the farm, overlooking historic Shawnee Springs, and the building was christened the Springhouse. The Andersons relished the beautiful view of the springs and ancient bald cypress trees in the valley below.

Exposing the structure of the barn, the engineers and craftsmen enclosed the facility in a glass skin and left the interior open except for bathroom and loft. During the year-long process of reconstruction, the team added a stone fireplace and minimal modern conveniences.

> The barn, which appeared
> to be a typical five-bent
> tobacco barn, was actually
> a yellow poplar,
> mortise-and-tenon
> structure with joints
> connected by tapered pegs.

The interior plan, which was formulated by Ruth Anderson and Cincinnati designer David Millet, features unpainted surfaces, unfinished beams and walls, and pegged oak floors. Shaker and period type furniture, as well as family quilts, decorate the house.

Since the Springhouse was finished in 1991, it has welcomed guests from all over the world.

The Schuller Cabin

The Schuller Cabin
and the Crystal Cathedral

When Ralph G. Anderson learned that an 1825 log structure in Metcalfe County was in danger of being demolished, he purchased the building and had it reassembled on Anderson Circle land near Shawnee Springs.

While visiting the farm, Ralph and Ruth's dear friend, Dr. Robert H. Schuller, commented that the log cabin and its tranquil setting provided the ideal author's retreat. The one-room structure was immediately christened the Schuller Cabin, in honor of the founding pastor of Crystal Cathedral Ministries in Garden Grove, California.

On a visit to the Crystal Cathedral soon after its completion in 1980, the Andersons were amazed by the massive star-shaped edifice constructed of 10,000 panels of glass. Ralph laughingly asked his friend, Robert H. Schuller, an Iowa farm boy, how much hay could be stored in the twelve-story cathedral. Reverend Schuller responded drolly, "You'd never fill it up!"

Today, Ralph Anderson, a 30-year member of the Crystal Cathedral Ministries Board of Directors, credits Robert Schuller with being a major influence on his positive outlook on life, and remains proud of the ministry's good work in reaching 45 million people around the world.

> "In the top ten of all the men I have known, including kings and presidents, Ralph G. Anderson would be included. His humility and honesty have given him the fine reputation he so richly deserves."
>
> *Robert H. Schuller,*
> *Founding Minister, Crystal Cathedral Ministries*

Ralph Anderson (left) and his wife, Ruth, often welcomed Dr. Robert H. Schuller to their home and were happy to provide him a retreat from the demands of his extensive ministry.

Every Hill and Valley Imbued with History

Visitors to Anderson Circle Farm often gasp in wonder at the magnificence of Walnut Hall or admire the long years of history evident in the logs of old barns. But there are dozens, perhaps hundreds, of historical sites on the farm that are less obvious yet perhaps equally central to the history of the common man in Kentucky.

In truth, nearly every hill and valley at Anderson Circle Farm seems to hold secrets of Kentucky history. Look across one pasture, and you may see a site that was sacred to Native Americans. Scan another valley, and you may find a generous spring with a blue tint that mesmerized frontiersmen.

Facts and legends abound on Anderson Circle's 7,000 acres. It is a place steeped in history and fortunate to be held under the watchful eye of Ralph G. Anderson, a devoted student of history and Kentucky heritage.

Spillman Farm and Shawnee Springs

The portion of Anderson Circle Farm known as the Spillman Farm is the site of Shawnee Springs, a center of Indian activity in the region's precolonial days. Two cypress trees that stand near the flowing water likely were used in Native American religious ceremonies. These beautiful springs, which James Harrod noticed on his first visit to the area, served as an important hunting area for the Shawnee Indians. Game regularly came to the springs for

> Two cypress trees that stand near the flowing water likely were used in Native American religious ceremonies.

water and adjacent salt licks. In the late 1770s, Hugh McGary erected a 'station' (a protected residence) near the springs, becoming the first of many colonial settlers to give Shawnee Springs added historical importance.

Fountain Blue

The 700-acre Fountain Blue (Fontainebleau) farm is known for its large flowing spring with a bluish-hued, sandy bottom. Archeological evidence reveals that Indians lived and hunted in this area, attracted to the constantly flowing spring. While other historic sites on Anderson

Circle Farm are traced through James Harrod and his party, the Fountain Blue spring site was originally claimed by one of Kentucky's first surveyors, Isaac Hite.

Added to Anderson Circle Farm in 1995, this fertile farm is recognized as the site of the cultivation of state's first domestic corn crop in the summer of 1774.

Froman House

Old Barns and Houses:
More than Meets the Eye

Just as water, one of the most common elements on Anderson Circle Farm, holds truths from the past, so do some of its unobtrusive buildings. In many instances, it took Ralph G. Anderson's watchful eye and historical knowledge to tell the difference between an eyesore ready for demolition and a historical gem worth preserving.

Froman House

In 1996, Ralph and Ruth purchased the Froman Farm and later realized that the dilapidated farmhouse had remarkable links to early Mercer County history.

While investigating the house after purchasing the land, Ralph became curious about the thick wall that stood between the living room and dining room. The fifteen-inch thickness was out of character for such a dwelling, and on further investigation he discovered rough-hewn logs.

That discovery led to subsequent research which revealed that the 1860 Jacob Froman farmhouse had, at its core, a 1783 one-room log structure that dates it as one of the earliest homes in Kentucky still standing on its original site.

The core dwelling had been enlarged several times to reach its present size and configuration featuring eleven rooms. The Anderson team took great care to restore part of the log portion to reveal details of construction from the original log cabin. The exposed yellow poplar logs are chinked with mud and horse hair mortar.

Overall, the home has been repaired and modernized to become the residence of a farm employee.

Shaker Barn

After the purchase of the Froman Farm in 1996, the Anderson Circle team discovered an old barn to the north of the house. Aware that members of the Shaker community owned the farm from 1811-1817, the team realized that the barn might have been constructed by expert Shaker craftsmen.

Most Shaker barns were long, rectangular structures, two or more stories tall and usually built into a hillside so they could be entered at different levels. Large earthen ramps allowed entry from each level, and the foundation was usually constructed of randomly laid limestone. A massive stone wall runs the interior length of this Shaker barn to provide stability and separation of animals.

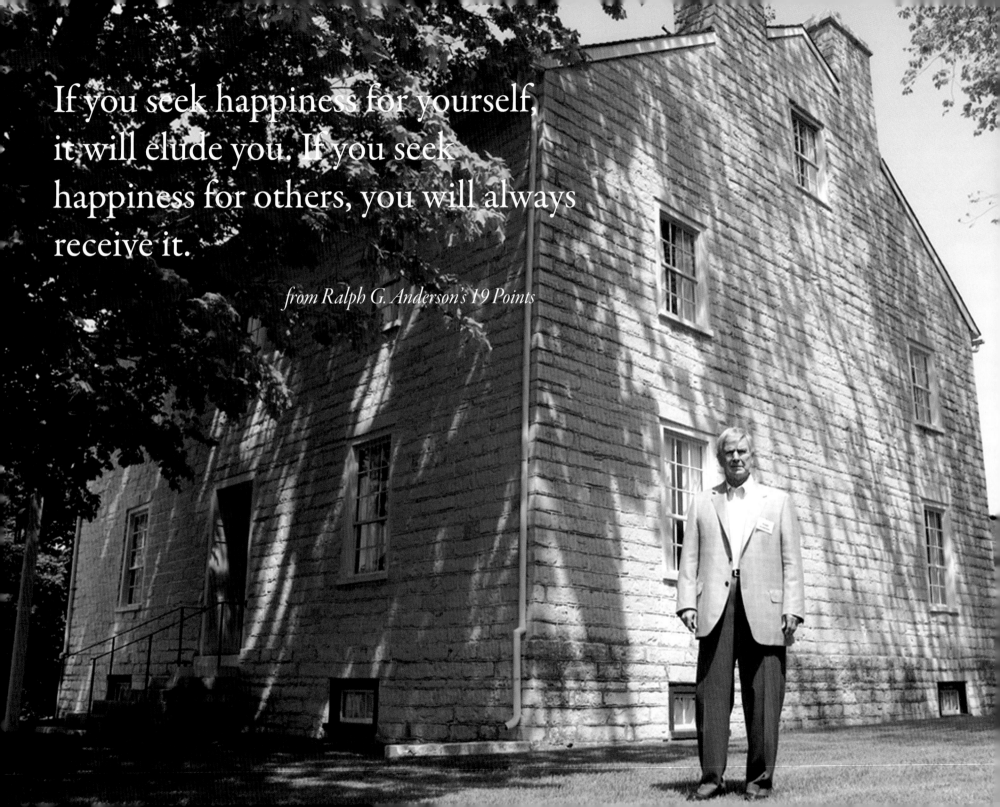

If you seek happiness for yourself, it will elude you. If you seek happiness for others, you will always receive it.

from Ralph G. Anderson's 19 Points

A Giving Heart

Funds generated by hard work spin off to transform a region

The amazing success of the Belcan Corporation over the past fifty years has allowed Ralph G. Anderson to support many causes close to his heart. As a philanthropist, Ralph is a wonderful paradox, a man with the mind of an engineer and the soul of a dreamer. He has a passion for preserving natural resources and historical landmarks, yet he remains at the forefront of cutting-edge technology.

When a charitable project requires expertise in engineering, Ralph does not hesitate to call on the many well-versed employees at Belcan. The combined power of his financial gifts and expertise has transformed people, places, and ideas in his beloved Mercer County and far beyond. Ralph has been a generous patron of historic preservation projects, engineering education, religious organizations, and community development.

Hundreds of people have benefited from this spirit of generosity, ranging from kids playing softball in their favorite park to actors taking the stage for a community drama production.

The Belcan CEO has been a patron of historic preservation projects, educational institutions, religious organizations, and community development.

The Future of Engineering:
Mentor to a New Generation

Ralph G. Anderson believes that students are worth supporting, particularly engineering students. Belcan is involved with colleges and universities around the country in offering co-op opportunities to students and aspiring engineers. Students are often paired with an experienced engineer, who serves as a mentor as the team completes various projects.

Through this program and others, he has assisted schools including the University of Cincinnati (engineering scholarships), Brigham Young University (PACE project Formula One race car), the University of Kentucky (solar car), a college and university consortium (KySAT), and Kentucky Community and Technical College System (scholarships at Gateway and Bluegrass).

Ralph has an especially strong relationship with the University of Kentucky, where he earned a bachelor of science degree in mechanical engineering in 1950. More than forty years after he served as a student supervisor in the engineering machine shop, Ralph was inducted in 1993 into the College of Engineering Hall of Distinction. One year later, he was awarded an Honorary Doctor of Engineering by his alma mater.

On UK's campus today, the Ralph G. Anderson Building (photo at left), dedicated in 2002,

completes the College of Engineering Quadrangle and serves as a monument to Ralph's continuing support of his alma mater.

Ralph, along with his late wife Ruth, their daughter Candace McCaw, and three grandchildren are University of Kentucky Fellows.

Examples of his support include formulation of a master plan for the UK College of Engineering, one that is followed today. Ralph also commissioned a massive bas relief carving of the University's facilities. Located in the main administration

building, the sculpture includes a depiction of Bacon College (1839), an early Mercer County institution that was re-organized in 1857 as the University of Kentucky.

A Sense of Gratitude:
'Lucky and proud to call him our own'

When our historians document those alumni who have dramatically and positively impacted the University of Kentucky, Ralph G. Anderson will be at the top of the list. He is a great personal friend and counselor for me, as well as the students who study in the engineering building named for him.

Mr. Anderson's Belcan Corporation has been providing leading-edge engineering services and solutions to clients since 1958. Lexington

is especially fortunate to have such a great partnership with the company, and UK is very lucky and proud to call him one of our own.

Dr. Lee T. Todd, Jr.
President
University of Kentucky

KySAT: Students Meet Satellites

Ralph G. Anderson has succeeded in business and in life by pursuing innovation, and he enjoys supporting forward-thinking projects that involve future generations of engineers. He has been a patron of KySAT, an ambitious collaboration among the state's public universities and community college system, as well as government agencies and private funding sources. This student-led initiative is focused on design and construction required for launching and operating small satellites and other spacecraft to promote scientific knowledge.

The Kentucky Satellite (KySAT) consortium was formed under the leadership of the Kentucky Science and Technology Corporation, and has close ties with several divisions at the NASA Ames Research Center.

KySat's ultimate goal is to solicit public and private payloads for an on-going series of launches of near-space, sub-orbital and orbital missions. Belcan supports the project with engineering expertise and other funding.

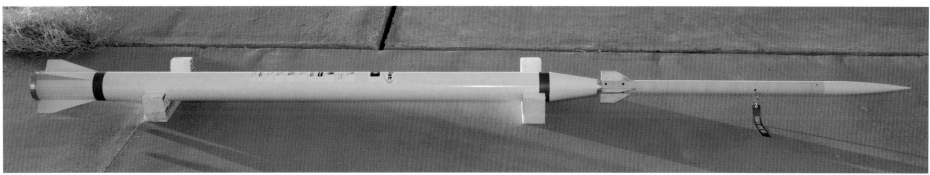

Kentucky Agriculture Heritage Center: Preserving the Past, Ensuring the Future

Ralph G. Anderson has always been a man capable of bringing together that which is practical with that which is visionary. He is both a farmer and engineer, and in the summer of 2005, he and his farm manager, Harvey Mitchell, convened a meeting to talk with members of the Kentucky agriculture community. Ralph wanted to explore with them his commitment to farming, preservation of the rural lifestyle, and possible applications of cutting-edge technology.

That meeting led to others as the group explored the feasibility of and level of interest in a Kentucky agriculture museum. With the support and involvement of many farm and commodity groups, the initial planning phase of the project continued until the summer of 2006.

> Ralph Anderson wanted to talk with other members of the agriculture community, exploring his commitment to farming, preservation of the rural lifestyle, and possible applications of cutting-edge technology.

> Scheduled to open in 2010, the center was designed by Belcan architect Isaac Gilliam and his team to be a model in sustainable design, utilizing wind, solar, geothermal, and other alternative power sources.

After an invitation to every county in Kentucky to submit a proposal for the location of the facility, and after months of study and site visits, the group chose Mercer County as home of the new Kentucky Agriculture Heritage Center.

Ralph Anderson donated fifty acres of land from the Anderson Circle Farm, a working farmstead, the services of his Belcan technology and architectural staff, and pledges of continuing support to make the project a reality. To complement Ralph's generous gift, Mercer County and Harrodsburg pledged valuable infrastructure support.

The Kentucky Agriculture Heritage Center was designed by Belcan architect Isaac Gilliam and his team as a model project for sustainable design. Utilizing wind, solar, geothermal, and other alternative power sources, the 300,000 square-foot facility is projected to include a conference center and exhibition halls, an Agriculture Hall of Fame gallery, educational classrooms, indoor and outdoor cooking facilities, and an alternative energy demonstration pavilion.

Dedicated to providing farmers with alternative strategies for improving production and reducing costs, the Kentucky Agriculture Heritage Board promotes an ambitious mission: *The Kentucky Agriculture Heritage Center will create an environment for learning, reflecting on the past, showcasing the present, and fostering the advancement of Kentucky agriculture.*

Scheduled to open in 2010, the Kentucky Agriculture Heritage Center and Ralph G. Anderson maintain similar philosophies: preserving the best of the past and ensuring a successful future.

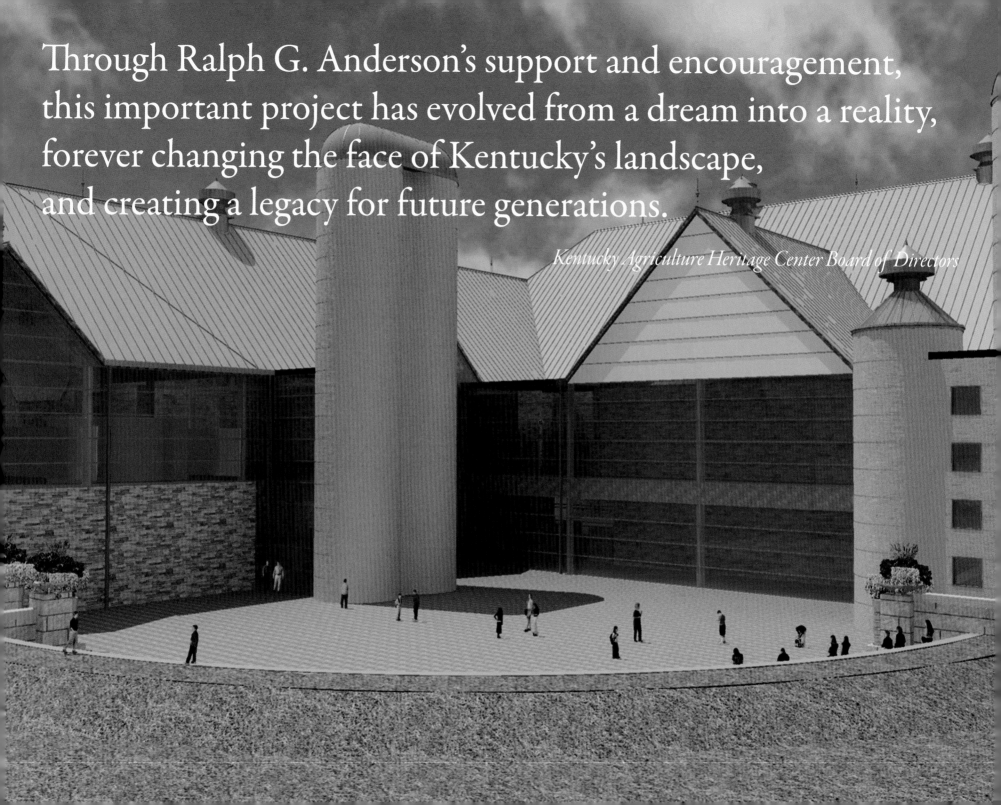

Through Ralph G. Anderson's support and encouragement, this important project has evolved from a dream into a reality, forever changing the face of Kentucky's landscape, and creating a legacy for future generations.

Kentucky Agriculture Heritage Center Board of Directors

Agriculture in Kentucky: Quick Facts

Agriculture remains important in Kentucky, according to statistics released in 2007 by the U.S. Department of Agriculture.

- Top five agricultural exports from Kentucky (valued at more than $1.2 billion):
  Tobacco
  Live animals and meat
  Feed grains
  Soybeans
  Poultry

- Top commodities, by dollar value:
  Horses and mules
  Cattle and calves
  Broilers
  Corn
  Soybeans

- Top five counties in agricultural sales:
  Fayette
  Woodford
  Graves
  Bourbon
  Webster

- 18% of all jobs in state directly connected to farming

- 54% of the state's land area is designated as farmland (13.84 million acres out of 25.43 million)

- Number of farms: 84,000

- Average farm size: 160 acres

- 91.6 percent of Kentucky farms are owned by families or individuals

- Average age of farmers: 55.2

- Crop output: over $1.3 billion

- Animal output: $2.7 billion

- Services/forestry output: $1.07 billion

- Total agricultural output valued at more than $5.2 billion

Kentucky Department of Agriculture Website

USDA.gov/StateFacts/KY 7/2008

KentuckyHistoricalSociety
Keeping Promises for Kentucky History
Hats Off to Kentucky History!
Join the Celebration • July 9, 2005
Thomas D. Clark Center
KENTUCKY

Preserving and Celebrating
the History of the Commonwealth

The history of Kentucky is filled with larger-than-life figures ranging from frontiersman Daniel Boone to Supreme Court Justice John Marshall Harlan. On the list of Kentucky's modern history heroes, Dr. Thomas Dionysius Clark ranks at the forefront.

Dr. Clark's seventy-year association with the University of Kentucky History Department and his active role in promoting and preserving the history of the Commonwealth led to his designation as Kentucky Historian Laureate for Life. Blessed with longevity, a keen mind, and a spirit of community activism, he authored more than thirty books and involved himself in numerous projects.

Dr. Clark was a driving force behind the 1999 opening of a state-of-the-art Kentucky History Center in Frankfort, which serves as headquarters for the Kentucky Historical Society, a museum, library, and archival center. He was honored in 2005 when the Center was renamed the Thomas D. Clark Center for Kentucky History. Kentucky's revered historian died just two weeks before his 102nd birthday.

Ralph G. Anderson maintains a strong admiration for Dr. Clark and pledged a substantial gift to the Thomas D. Clark Education Challenge Fund, The Campaign for Kentucky, which supports the Historical Society's educational projects.

"Ralph G. Anderson's love for
Kentucky is an inspiration to us
all and his personal success story
is a great piece of Kentucky and
business history in its own right!"

Kent Whitworth
Executive Director,
Kentucky Historical Society

Today, Anderson remains active in the Kentucky Historical Society as a member of the Lincoln Society at the Chancellor's Friends level. He says simply, "I contribute to the Historical Society because its mission is important."

Shaker Village of Pleasant Hill: Buildings Restored and History Brought Alive

The connection of Ralph G. Anderson to Shaker Village of Pleasant Hill epitomizes a near-perfect match between a donor and a charitable cause. Ralph has a passion for history, agriculture, and his native Mercer County. Shaker Village represents all three. Founded as a religious colony in the 1800s, the Village also led the region in agricultural experimentation and growth. The residents were gifted craftsman, and their buildings, furniture, and implements held an artistry that still is admired.

Eager to help professional staff members at the Village in their efforts to preserve Shaker heritage, Ralph brought to bear many resources from Belcan Corporation, according to Jim Thomas, the retired Shaker Village CEO.

> Eager to help
> professional staff members
> in their efforts
> to preserve Shaker heritage,
> Ralph brought to bear
> many resources
> from Belcan Corporation.

The Belcan staff assisted in organizing and digitizing the Village's collection of documents, along with photos of artifacts and buildings. The collection has been installed on a new Belcan-designed and hosted web site.

"The IT project significantly brought Shakertown into the twenty-first century," says Thomas. "We couldn't afford computer hardware or software. The expert Belcan staff came here and installed a high-speed T-1 line and a new phone system."

The Belcan engineering staff surveyed Shakertown's land and created a map of the 3,000 acres. "For the first time," notes Thomas, "we knew exactly where our boundaries were."

Another of Anderson's initiatives required some personal risk-taking. Pleasant Hill depends heavily on tourism to generate its operating income, and for years the dining facilities were hampered by a countywide prohibition against alcohol. Although other businesses and citizens had tried in past years to get a referendum passed allowing limited alcohol sales in Shakertown's dining areas, those had failed. The tide turned with Anderson's encouragement.

Thomas explains: "Ralph went out on a limb and made known his wishes to give Shakertown and Harrodsburg's Beaumont Inn the option to serve adult beverages. He felt strongly that if you were in the hospitality business, you couldn't have one hand tied behind your back. He provided the funding and impetus to take a stand in the community. It wasn't popular with all citizens, but he stood with us the whole way." As a result, through a local referendum, Shakertown and Beaumont Inn may serve alcohol at their respective restaurants.

At another point in his support of Shaker Village, Ralph purchased a farm that adjoined Pleasant Hill. In danger of becoming a housing development, the land that was originally a part of the Shaker Village, is now a conference center and a series of walking and riding trails meandering through the unique Kentucky countryside.

"In a board meeting, they said the farm next door, which had been an old Shaker farm, was being put up for sale," Ralph recalls. "They were afraid of what might go. I rely on intuition, and on the way home, I said, 'I can buy that and give it to them.' Had to borrow the money, but I did it."

> "Belcan's contributions have allowed us to compete more effectively in today's hospitality industry."
>
> *Madge B. Adams*
> *President, Shaker Village of Pleasant Hill*

A Brief History of the Shakers

Founded as a religious communal society, the "Shaking Quakers" earned their name from animated movements exhibited as an element of the group's religious services. By the 1840s, nearly 3,500 Shakers lived in communities from Maine to Kentucky. A group arrived in Central Kentucky around 1805 and established Pleasant Hill village.

Experts in agriculture, the sect created new breeds of sheep, chickens, and cattle; in fact, Shaker brethren were asked to be cattle judges at Kentucky's state fair. In addition to the cultivation of 3,000 acres of wheat, rye, oats, and flax, as well as fruit orchards, the brethren made brooms, coopers ware, weaving implements, and shoes, while the sisters produced woolen goods, cheese, and preserves.

The Shaker population peaked at almost 500 in the 1820s, but after the 1860s, changing social attitudes and the Industrial Revolution signaled the community's decline. After the last Shaker was gone, the buildings, property, and furnishings were dispersed to private owners.

In early 1961, a groundswell of interest in saving the historic Shaker structures led to the formation of a nonprofit, educational corporation, Shakertown at Pleasant Hill, Kentucky, Inc., and by 1968, the first section of the recreated village had opened. Today, America's largest restored Shaker community exhibits thirty-four carefully-restored buildings and 3,000 acres of preserved farmland in a living history setting. Ralph G. Anderson has been a member of the Shakertown Board of Directors for twenty years. In the words of Jim Thomas, retired President and CEO of the Shaker Village, "Ralph Anderson is a very intelligent and successful man with no pretensions at all. He's a workhorse, not a showhorse."

DIAMOND
POINT
WELCOME CENTER

A History Worth Preserving: Birthplace of the West

Mercer County was an important hub in the settlement of the West. Often referred to as the "Birthplace of the West," the county seat, Harrodsburg, hosted many pioneers on their journeys to settle the Western frontier. In 1774, James Harrod traveled down the Kentucky River, camped at a beautiful spring, and founded "Harrod's Town," the first permanent English settlement west of the Allegheny Mountains.

Locals are fond of saying that the history of the county is as rich as the soil. Mercer County's 250 square miles showcase beautiful farmland, gently rolling countryside, and historic stone fences.

Kentucky's oldest town claims a proud and remarkable heritage. Legendary figures

> Kentucky's oldest town claims a proud heritage. Legendary figures including Daniel Boone and James Harrod played a role in the history of this Central Kentucky county.

including Robert McAfee, Daniel Boone, and James Harrod played a role in the rich history of this Central Kentucky Bluegrass county.

In modern times, Ralph G. Anderson's name is honored and recognized here. The native son owns Anderson Circle Farm, one of the state's largest working farms.

Over the years, the Andersons have supported numerous civic projects in Harrodsburg and Mercer County, including construction-restoration of historic buildings, websites for nonprofit organizations, and the Anderson-Dean Community Park.

Working collaboratively with his expert Belcan staff, Ralph has been responsible for saving and preserving dozens of buildings, archives, collections, and monuments.

Ralph's late wife, Ruth, loved the Harrodsburg community and its citizens. She was known for bringing attention to worthy local projects with her themed fundraising parties. In 1992, the Andersons began hosting gala balls and events for the Ragged Edge Community Theatre and other local charities. Ruth would often appear in a specially-designed 1840's ballgown, greeting her guests with customary warmth and enthusiasm. As one guest recalls: "Ruth loved knowing the people of Harrodsburg. The Andersons were a very happy, fun couple to be around."

Joining a group of Mercer County's most esteemed citizens, Ralph became a founding member of the James Harrod Trust Advisory Board in 1999. This group of Mercer County citizens banded together to preserve local landmarks and maintains a mission of advocating for the historic preservation and heritage of the area.

Helen Dedman, who chairs the trust, is grateful to Ralph for preserving at least five historic homes in Mercer County, as well as rich, historic farmland. "Maintaining Anderson Circle Farm and keeping farmland in production," says Dedman, "helps us preserve Mercer County's beautiful countryside."

The Ruth M. Anderson Research Collection at the Mercer County Library is heavily used by area researchers and students.

Ralph G. Anderson has supported projects in Mercer County at the Fort Harrod historic site, which includes the replica of a stockade as well as the Lincoln Wedding Chapel (photos left and far left). He also has been a patron of James B. Haggin Hospital. Ruth Anderson made a major gift to the Mercer County Public Library in 1993, allowing the library to become the state's third repository for the Lyman Copeland Draper Research Collection (the other two are the Kentucky Historical Society and Louisville's Filson Club). This renowned collection, consisting of 123 reels of microfilm, details the history of early frontiersmen and families from 1755-1815. Today, the Ruth M. Anderson Research Collection is heavily used by area researchers and students. In addition to sponsoring the Draper Collection, Ruth donated hundreds of books to the library.

The 213-acre Anderson-Dean Park has become a central meeting place for Mercer countians.

A Park for the Young and the Young-at-Heart

"Every time I pass the Anderson-Dean Park on U.S. 127," says Mercer County Judge Executive John D. Trisler, "I think of Ralph and Ruth Anderson, along with their daughter, Candace McCaw, and their contributions to so many children, youth and adults from Mercer County."

Trisler recalls an early series of events that illustrates Ralph G. Anderson's generosity. The Andersons hosted a park board planning meeting at their farm in the mid 1990s. "During the meeting," Trisler says, "Ralph tugged at my sleeve and told me we were not planning enough parking spaces. I told him we didn't have any more space."

The story did not end there, according to the Mercer executive. "In ten days or so, I received a call from Ralph, who indicated that he had purchased the farm that adjoined the park, and he wished to donate it. This doubled our park size and provided for one of the best recreational areas in the state."

The 213-acre Anderson-Dean Park, located three miles from Harrodsburg, was developed in 1993 with financing from city/county government, private donations and state grants. Today, the park is a central meeting place for Mercer countians.

The list of activity areas includes an aquatic center and a skate park (photos left and above), playgrounds, tennis courts, other pavilions and athletic courses. Recently, Ralph and his daughter Candace funded the Ruth Anderson Softball Complex and a state-of-the art skateboard park.

"Every time I pass the park,
I think of Ralph and Ruth
Anderson, and their daughter
Candace."

103

The Blue Front Theatre: A Hub of Activity in the 1880s

Architectural gems abound on Main Street in Harrodsburg, Kentucky, but even in a town filled with remarkable structures, the Blue Front Theatre is distinctive. The blue-painted concrete exterior, a tower topped with a turret, and multiple stone-arched entrances give the sense that this building is one-of-a-kind.

Despite its charm, the Blue Front had fallen into a state of disrepair by the mid-1980s. Ralph G. Anderson's passion for historic buildings prompted him into action in 1988. Belcan's design team entered the condemned building and immediately became concerned about serious structural issues.

The building's facade seemed on the verge of collapsing into an adjoining street. Sagging roof

> The second floor of the Blue Front housed a theater in the 1880s. Utilized by theater troupes and civic groups, the auditorium was a hub of activity in early Harrodsburg.

trusses left a gap of thirteen inches between the Blue Front's masonry wall and the main structure.

After making an exhaustive study of the building and bringing together the needed experts, the Belcan team devised a way to save the building. Workers inserted tension rods into the steel framing of the building next door, reducing the gap and stabilizing the Blue Front.

Through historical research, the group discovered that the second floor of the Blue Front had housed a theater in the 1880s. Utilized by traveling theater troupes and civic groups, the auditorium had been a hub of activity for early Harrodsburg.

After renovation of the first floor for the offices of the Harrodsburg Eye Center, the renovation team turned to restoration of the second floor theater. Sixty percent of the plaster was gone, the original stage was missing, and the balcony sagged, reducing the old theater to a sad shell that showed little promise.

Even so, the determined team caught intriguing glimpses of the building's past character and glittering life. There were colorful wall designs, a ceiling painted to create the effect of moon and stars, and a scattering of old playbills. In a true testament to Ralph G. Anderson's commitment to preservation, the Belcan CEO made a commitment to restoring this historic treasure.

"This theater is a work of art, much like a painting."
—Isaac Gilliam, Belcan Vice President and Chief Architect

During eighteen months of restoration, a Belcan team commissioned experts to meticulously study plaster, paint, and the few remaining designs from the highly decorated theater. Kris Lemmon's DecoWorks team, experts in restoration painting, conducted meticulous paint and design analysis. Woods and molding patterns were researched, and local construction expert Gary Lay was commissioned to handcraft woodwork, doors, and window trims.

Now replete with a restored balcony and stage, the theater stands as a work of art. It is embellished with 144 colors and numerous decorative designs. Due to structural code restrictions, usage of the second floor theater will be limited, but Ralph proudly conducts tours of one his most decorative restorations.

Home Away from Home:
The Beaumont Inn

Ralph G. Anderson has a special place in his heart for the historic Beaumont Inn in Harrodsburg and the Dedman family that owns and operates it. For Ralph, a room at the Inn and a meal in its venerable dining room is guaranteed to create the feel of a home away from home.

The Dedmans make it clear that the warm feelings are mutual between the two Mercer County families.

"Ralph has become a part of our family here at Beaumont. We are honored that he considers us his 'home away from home.' His support and encouragement means so much to our inn and the economic health of one of Kentucky's most historic communities."

Chuck Dedman
Owner, Beaumont Inn

1860 Dedman's Drugstore, Harrodsburg, KY

The Belcan Impact in Mercer County: From a Frontier Fort to Digital Archives

Generous support from Ralph G. Anderson and Belcan Corporation has impacted multiple sites and projects in Mercer County.

Anderson Circle Farm historic building restorations
Anderson-Dean Park, including softball field, skateboard facility, and swimming pool
Blue Front Restoration, including Theater
1860 Dedman's Drugstore
Ford Harrod drama
Harrodsburg First (website)
Harrodsburg Tourism (PC support)
Harrodsburg Visitors' Bureau (video)
Hat Factory
James B. Haggin Memorial Hospital
James Harrod Trust (website)
Kentucky Agriculture Heritage Center (land and building design)
Local churches
Mercer County Fairgrounds
Mercer County Planning Commission
Mercer County Public Library
Mudd Meeting House
Ragged Edge Theater
Rocky Pointe restoration
Shaker Village of Pleasant Hill

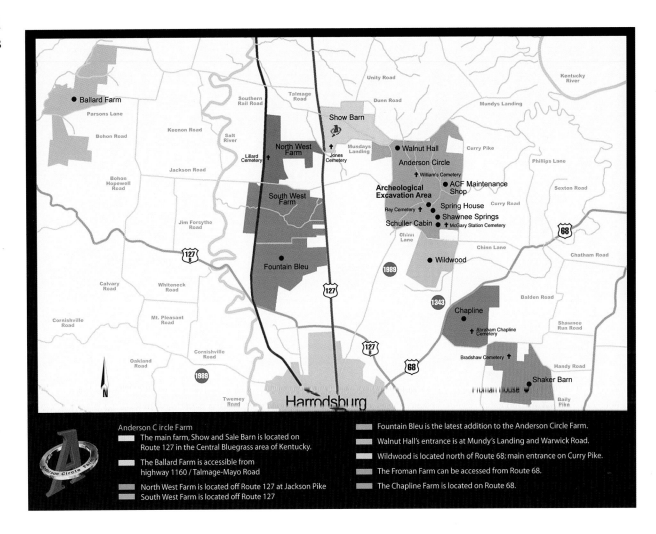

Anderson Circle Farm

The main farm, Show and Sale Barn is located on Route 127 in the Central Bluegrass area of Kentucky.

The Ballard Farm is accessible from highway 1160 / Talmage-Mayo Road

North West Farm is located off Route 127 at Jackson Pike
South West Farm is located off Route 127

Fountain Bleu is the latest addition to the Anderson Circle Farm.

Walnut Hall's entrance is at Mundy's Landing and Warwick Road.

Wildwood is located north of Route 68; main entrance on Curry Pike.

The Froman Farm can be accessed from Route 68.

The Chapline Farm is located on Route 68.

Belcan owners, corporate staff, and managers from across
the United States gather at the corporation's headquarters
in Cincinnati, Ohio for this August, 2008 photo.

Today and Tomorrow: The Legacy Continues

A spirit of vitality makes the future look bright

The United States welcomed a number of cultural icons in 1958, the year Belcan was chartered. The first Bic ballpoint pen appeared that year, along with Jiffy Pop and Barbie. The Platters produced an album that became perennially popular, *Smoke Gets in Your Eyes*, and Tommy Edwards' number 1 hit, *It's All in the Game*, proved to have staying power.

> Who could have predicted that Belcan eventually would achieve a ten percent annual growth rate and sustain it for decades, becoming one of the largest privately-owned engineering corporations in the nation?

Even so, the business climate did not bode well for a new company. Start-ups that year had a failure rate around fifty-six percent. Belcan's gross revenue for the first three years—an unimpressive $200—did not seem to buck the trend. Who could have predicted that Belcan eventually would achieve a ten percent annual growth rate and sustain it for decades, becoming one of the largest privately-owned engineering corporations in the nation?

The answers lie in Belcan's founder and CEO, Ralph G. Anderson, and the strong team he assembled. At the time of the company's founding, he relied on hard work, intuition, and an absolute commitment to excellence. Today, he maintains that personal philosophy and has the quiet assurance of a self-made man.

Ralph enjoys listening to the motivational tapes of Wayne Dyer and agrees with Dyer's straightforward personal philosophy: "There is no such thing as stress. It's the way you process it in your mind. If something happens you can do something about, do it. If not, forget it."

(continued on page 115)

The Wisdom of Anderson

"Cycles go in three's," says Ralph Anderson. "It takes three years to realize a profit, three years to build a relationship, three years to break even." With that theory in mind, anyone planning a new business venture should be realistic about the time and money required for start-up. Belcan bookkeepers have been amazed at Ralph's ability to closely estimate and approximate the numbers they would eventually record.

111

Wisdom Condensed: The 19 Points

Belcan is a business with an incredibly strong foundation and the strength to thrive in the future. The source of that strength can be traced directly to the business philosophy and personal convictions of Ralph G. Anderson, which took root in his childhood and were formalized in a 1995 document known as *19 Points*. These statements have such clear and enduring value that new Belcan staff members now receive a copy during employee orientation.

Ralph G. Anderson's

1 If you have a problem, it's because of how you think. And the only way that you can ever fix a problem is to change your thinking.

2 If you have a choice of being right or being kind, always choose kind. You always have a choice.

3 Be part of the solution, not the problem. If you are not part of the solution then you are part of the problem.

4 There is no stress; it is the way you process it in your mind.

5 Trust in your intuition.

6 Negative thoughts tear you down; positive thoughts build you up.

7 Your opinion of me is none of my business.

8 When you judge a person you define yourself; you want them to be like you.

9 When you let others people's opinion of you bother you, you let them control you. You have no control of other people's opinion; you have control of your character.

19 Points

10   People don't care how smart you are until they find out how much you care.

11   EGO = Edging God Out.

12   You get treated in life the way you teach people to treat you. If you fight them they fight back; if you give love then you will receive love back.

13   If you seek happiness for yourself it will always elude you. If you seek happiness for others, you will always receive it.

14   Listen. You can't learn anything by talking.

15   Be a leader. One who looks at the overall picture of the company, not just a part of the company.

16   A leader doesn't care who gets the credit.

17   You control your thoughts, your thoughts control your emotions; therefore, you control your emotions — don't blow up.

18   We live to be happy and to have fun. It's all internal.

19   This is my way. What is your way? *The way* does not exist.

Principles for Business and for Life

**"Every setback in life has ended up
teaching me something."**

Ralph G. Anderson is certain that a person—or a business—can learn a great deal from life's negatives. He points to Henry Ford, who said that failure was simply an opportunity to begin again, more intelligently.

**"Invest in the capital, land, and building
before attempting to secure a contract.
Stick your neck out, show you're ready, and
the business will come to you."**

Ralph has habitually taken the risk of obtaining facilities before a successful contract was negotiated. He believes that demonstrating the capability to do the job is the precursor to a signature on a contract.

**"Companies' reputations are built
on delivering. Not just promising,
but delivering services."**

Belcan takes pride in a company policy which dictates that project teams must meet every deadline and budget projection.

"Raise them up."

Employing a country term for childrearing, 'Raising them up,' Ralph believes in linking fresh graduates with experienced professionals. Paul Ross, Belcan's Corporate Recruiting Manager, explains: "At any given moment, we always have several recent graduates on site for mentoring. We also maintain co-op rotations for engineering students from the University of Cincinnati, University of Kentucky, University of Louisville, Ohio State, and Purdue University."

Ralph has always valued family ties and takes great pride in the McCaw family. Seen above with daughter, Candace Anderson McCaw.

Friends who inquire about his well-being
are met with a smile and an enthusiastic answer:
"TRE...MENDOUS!"

Ralph G. Anderson
Awards & Honors

1954 State of Ohio Registered Professional Engineer
        Seal Number 21409

1992 University of Kentucky College of Engineering
        Outstanding Alumnus of the Year

1993 University of Kentucky College of Engineering
        Hall of Distinction

1995 University of Kentucky
        Hall of Distinguished Alumni

1995 University of Kentucky
        Honorary Ph.D. in Engineering

1995 Outstanding Alumnus of Kentucky
        OAK Award

That attitude was put to the test during the summer of 2006. Belcan was continuing to thrive, but not with the same spirit of vitality provided by the daily presence of the chief executive. Ralph's illness required a seven-month hospital stay, followed by recuperation at home and then a period of abbreviated work days.

As he was dealing with his own health crisis, Ralph G. Anderson lost his mate of almost 58 years, his beloved Ruth. The Anderson family had endured several difficult years as Ruth's health declined, and friends noted the remarkable dedication of Ralph and Candace during Ruth's long illness. Continuing the commitment he made years before, Ralph provided the best of care to the woman who had been his partner in business and his partner in life, Ruth.

Today, Ralph has returned to good health and continues his daily oversight of Belcan Corporation. He maintains a busy schedule of conferences, philanthropic board meetings, business luncheons and dinners, and weekend visits to his beloved Mercer County Anderson Circle Farm. Those who know Ralph G. Anderson can't imagine him retiring, playing golf, or fishing...for very long. Those activities wouldn't be as much fun as running Belcan. The CEO advises that if you go to work to have fun, you'll do a better job, and he has demonstrated that philosophy on a daily basis for the past 50 years.

The Belcan owner, chairman, and CEO maintains an open-door policy to all employees and answers his own telephone. His assistant, Vicki Jenkins, observes, "He constantly monitors billability, follows the numbers, and regularly keeps an eye on how the company is doing."

Ralph G. Anderson takes great pride in his family, often enjoying dinner with his daughter and son-in-law, Candace and Mike McCaw, and grandchildren, Jason, Matthew, and Amanda. The Kenwood Country Club staff members, whom Ralph views as extended family, often see him for lunch and dinner and instinctively know what he is likely to order.

Greeting the CEO of Belcan, those who inquire about his wellbeing are met with a smile and an enthusiastic answer: "TRE...MENDOUS!" Hale and hearty in his mid-eighties, Ralph Anderson eagerly anticipates the success of Belcan's next 50 years. Above all, he remains an inspiration to everyone who knows him.

Belcan for the next 50 years ... the story of success continues.

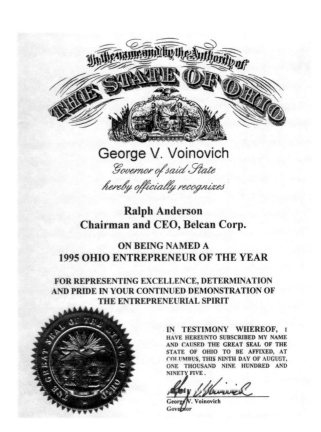

At a Glance: Belcan in 2008

- Founder/Owner/CEO: Ralph G. Anderson

- Founded in 1958 in Cincinnati, Ohio

- Current headquarters: Cincinnati

- Mission: A global service provider with 60 offices and locations around the world. Services are provided in every state and many foreign countries through a network of locations.

- Annual sales approaching $500 million

- Over 8,000 employees worldwide

- Services including:

  Full-Service Engineering

  Design and Build

  Application Technology

  Procurement

  Information Technology

  Technical and Temporary Staffing

  Multimedia

- Belcan ranks among the 500 largest engineering firms in the United States

- Belcan ranks among the 100 largest privately-owned engineering firms in the United States.

PHOTOS: Original photos of Anderson Circle Farm, Belcan Cincinnati location, Mercer County, Shaker Village at Pleasant Hill and the University of Kentucky by Ben Richardson. Other photos contributed by Belcan Corporation, the Anderson family, and the Kentucky Historical Society.